CORGIS

A Dog Training Guide about Pembroke Welsh Corgi and Cardigan Welsh Corgi for Beginners

By

Joseph Lint

in this book.

By reading this document, the reader agrees that under no circumstances is the author responsible for any losses, direct or indirect, which are incurred as a result of the use of information contained within this document, including, but not limited to, — errors, omissions, or inaccuracies.

Table of Contents

INTRODUCTION

Among the absolute cutest of all the dog breeds, corgis give new meaning to the word adorable. Corgis have become one of the more popular breeds in the last few years, due mostly to the prevalence of adorable photos and GIFs being shared across the internet. It is hard not to want a corgi once you see the way they wiggle their butt when excited, or the way their tongue flops around as their stubby little legs pump beneath them. Corgis are easily within the top five types of dog when it comes to popularity, so it comes as no surprise that you're here reading this book to prepare for adopting one of your own.

While the cuteness of these dogs is known by all, how much else do you know about them? Did you know that they are Queen Elizabeth's favorite type of dog? Or how about the fact that they were once used to herd cattle? You probably knew they are happy furballs, but did you know they love to receive attention, and they will work hard to please their masters? Despite the fact they have small bodies, corgis behave like much bigger dogs, and so it is important that you understand the ins and outs of this breed before adopting.

Corgis take well to training, so long as they receive it early enough. If you leave a corgi alone, then it will figure out how to train you instead. Corgis quickly get set in their ways, and undisciplined or untrained corgis are notorious for forming their own sets of behaviors, timelines, and rules. As these rules become habitual, a corgi will become even more stubborn and reluctant to accept changes. This means that you, as an owner, should know how to train your corgi before you adopt. If you wait to learn how to train them after they've entered the family, you may end up taking too much time and finding the experience more frustrating than you imagined. Corgis might take well to training, but they aren't as adaptable as a golden retriever or a border collie. Corgis can learn how to hold some minor job positions, but they aren't so flexible as to work as drug sniffers or hunting dogs, although they can be taught to be watchdogs or offer emotional support.

In this book, we will be covering everything you need to know to make adopting a corgi as smooth and drama-free as possible. Chapter one will begin by examining the history, traits, and characteristics of corgis before moving onto the pros and cons of adopting your own. Chapter two will build upon this information to determine if it is better to adopt a Pembroke Welsh corgi or a Cardigan Welsh corgi. We change gears in chapter three to look at how to set up and prepare your house for a corgi so that it doesn't cause messes, break valuables, or get into harmful chemicals or food stores.

Together, these three chapters take you from considering adopting through to a home ready for your new corgi.

The next chapter will commence the second section of the book, in which a corgi is now a member of your family, and you will be required to take care of them. Chapter four will cover grooming a corgi, from brushing to bathing, trimming to shedding; this chapter has everything you need to keep your furball looking clean and gorgeous. Chapter five will move to health and answer questions about a corgi's lifespan, common medical ailments, and hereditary diseases. Chapter five will also examine how to exercise and feed your corgi to keep them healthy and strong.

We move from issues of cleanliness and health and look at aspects of behavior with chapter six as we look at how well a corgi takes to training, and what basic commands they need to understand. There will also be a discussion on clicker training. Since training naturally invokes discipline, chapter seven will be looking at how we use reinforcement to create obedience rather than turning to physical abuse or threats. With the information in these chapters, you can make sure you are training your dog instead of your dog training you.

Chapter eight, the final chapter, will take a look at the life cycle of a corgi from puppy to adolescence through to adulthood. That will give you a timeline of what to expect from your dog so that you know the best time to train them (puppy), the point at which they will be the most frustrating (adolescence), and when they calm down into a mature, loving dog (adulthood). This short chapter will help you to slot the information from the rest of the book into a specific timeframe, which will help you to estimate requirements for training, exercise, and dieting.

It is my goal to provide you with everything you need to know to make adopting your corgi a hassle-free experience because everyone can use a little more corgi butt wiggling in their lives.

CHAPTER ONE

SHOULD YOU CHOOSE A CORGI AS YOUR DOG?

While the cuteness of a corgi might have you wanting to throw caution and preparation to the wind and adopt them right there on the spot, it is never a good idea to impulsively bring a new pet into your family. After all, a dog is, in many respects, a member of the family. You should know enough about your corgi to be able to say definitively whether or not you have the means to keep them healthy, train them, and provide them with enough company. If you don't know much about corgis yet, beyond that adorable smile of theirs, then you just don't have the necessary information to make an informed decision.

For one just example, did you know that not all corgis are the same? There are Pembroke Welsh corgis and Cardigan Welsh corgis, and, while both are cute, they're not the same thing. Corgi is a breed of canine,

1

but within each breed tends to be a couple of different varieties. Pembroke Welsh and Cardigan Welsh are the two varieties of corgi. If you didn't know that there were different types, then how could you say you are ready to adopt yet? Research and education are the keys to successfully integrating a new dog into your life, but by reading this book, you have already shown that you understand how valuable researching ahead of time is.

In this chapter, we will look at the history of both the Pembroke Welsh and the Cardigan Welsh corgi. By doing so, you'll come to find they have a much more fascinating history than you may have assumed. From there, we'll look at the traits and characteristics of this breed, and then we'll weigh the pros and cons so that you can make an informed decision on whether or not a corgi is right for you. If this chapter convinces you that a corgi isn't right for you, then that is okay; there are other breeds that may be a better fit. On the other hand, if this chapter doesn't dissuade you, then you should continue reading to the end to make sure there aren't any other red flags or deal-breakers, such as possible health concerns or limitations to their trainability.

The History of the Pembroke Welsh Corgi

When it comes to dog breeds, we have long and storied histories for most of them. Of course, this isn't always the case. If we take the golden retriever as an example, we see that golden retrievers didn't exist until the late 1800s, and so we have a short history of them. But we still have a history; we can trace golden retrievers back to the first retriever that was born with a golden coat and subsequently bred.

We aren't able to trace back the Pembroke Welsh corgi to its origin. In fact, if we really want to get into the history of the Pembroke Welsh corgi, then we need to enter into folklore. To do so, we leave behind the real world for a few moments. This isn't a unique activity in the world of history. When we study the history of Rome, for example, our understanding of how it was founded is entirely mythical. However, we still teach this in history classes because it helps us to understand the beliefs and legends of the time period or subject in question. In the academic world, this fusion of history with mythology is called "mythistoy." So rather than the unknown history of the Pembroke Welsh corgi, we must look at the mythistory behind these lovable furballs.

The myth behind the Pembroke Welsh corgi is that a pair of children was tending their cattle. They were commoners, yet they were on royal ground at the time of discovering a couple of puppies. At first, the children thought that the dogs were foxes. Since the animals were too young to be a threat to the farmers, the children showed these "foxes" compassion. Rather than kill them, as would have been appropriate for farmers concerned about their chicken coops, the children took these puppies home. Finding out they were dogs and not foxes, the children were told that they were a gift from the fairies. While this might seem an odd interpretation, Welsh folklore had many fairies in their stories, and they were said to use small dogs to pull their carts and carriages instead of horses. The way that corgis often have different colored fur around their shoulders was attributed to the saddles that the fairies put on them. Of course, this legend also ties into the fact that corgis were first used as cattle-herding dogs since the two children discovered them while tending to cattle.

While this legend is quite cute, it is easy to see that it doesn't represent reality quite so well. What it does represent is the way that Pembroke Welsh corgis were considered when they started to become a commonly raised breed. The legend also has some confusing elements, such as the mention of the children being on the King's land. This raises the question of whether or not the royalty or nobles had some hand in breeding these dogs or not. Unfortunately, we may never know the answer. So as far as we know, Pembroke Welsh corgis might actually be a gift from fairies to mankind.

However, there are some theories on the origin which are grounded in reality. One of the more widely supported theories is that the Pembroke Welsh corgi came to the British Isles through Viking raiders around the 10th century, maybe even earlier. One of the supporting pieces of evidence for this comes from the striking resemblance of the Pembroke Welsh corgi to the Swedish vallhund. This theory presumes that the Swedish vallhund was bred with dogs from the British Isles to create the Pembroke Welsh corgi. Another school of thought sees the origin as coming from the Flemish. In the 12th century, there were many weavers and other Flemish craftsmen that relocated to Pembrokeshire in Wales. This theory has it that it was Flemish dogs which were bred with Welsh dogs in order to result in the Pembroke Welsh corgi. However, there is no solid proof to verify if either the origin stories are true.

This difficulty even shows itself when we try to figure out the origin of the name corgi. There are clearly some Welsh roots within the word. "Cor" and "gi" could be taken from the words for "watch over" and "dog." If so, then "corgi" is merely a portmanteau. But there are arguments that the word comes from Celtic rather than Welsh. This camp argues that it was the Vikings that brought the word when they invaded. Yet another theory suggests that the name combines "dwarf" and "dog" as a portmanteau rather than "to gather" and "dog."

Whether we are speaking about the origin of the word corgi or the Pembroke Welsh corgi themselves, we hit a brick wall of competing theories. But, as we shall see, this is not the case when it comes to the Cardigan Welsh corgi.

The History of the Cardigan Welsh Corgi

While we don't know the history of the Pembroke Welsh Corgi, let us pretend, for a second, that the theory about the Viking raiders is correct. This theory posits the oldest of the origins by placing the Pembroke Welsh corgi's beginnings between the 8th and 10th centuries. This puts their birthday somewhere between 1100 and 1300 years ago. That's pretty old, but it's merely a puppy compared to the Cardigan Welsh corgi. If you want to talk about old breeds, the Cardigan Welsh corgi has been a part of Wales history for more than 3,000 years.

Cousins of the Dachshund, the Cardigan Welsh corgi arrived in Wales in aboriginal form long, long ago via Celtic tribes. To give you a sense of their place in history, aboriginal Cardigan Welsh corgis would serve alongside Celtic warriors in the battles against Roman legions. However, it should be noted that they were not bred for battle. Instead, they were intended to help with cattle. Cardigan Welsh corgis make fantastic cattle dogs since they are smart enough to herd them, but also scary enough to keep away predators or other animals trying to steal their master's livestock. For the Celtic tribes, who were often on the move, that made these dogs an essential worker. These were still aboriginal versions of the Cardigan Welsh corgis. It wouldn't be until later, when they were bred with local British breeds such as the sheepdog, that they started to develop into the dogs we think of today. The theory of the Pembroke Welsh corgi coming from the Vikings suggests that the Cardigan Welsh corgi was one of the dogs used to create the younger breed or corgis.

As dog shows became popular in the 1900s, corgis came to the public's attention. They were considered to be a single breed regardless of whether or not they were a Pembroke Welsh or a Cardigan Welsh. Since the distinction was ignored in the judges' eyes, people began to breed the two types together more often. Corgis began to cause quite a lot of frustration at these shows. One judge might favor a Pembroke over a Cardigan, while another was the reverse, and so the dogs would lose points for arbitrary reasons. It took them nine years to fix the category error, and place the two breeds into their own sections. This must have been a great relief to many. Also, the British Royal family decided to begin keeping Pembroke Welsh corgis. It is likely that the Cardigan Welsh corgi was being overlooked by the judges more often than the Pembrokes were.

The Cardigan Welsh corgi made it to America in the 1930s. There was a period in time when the genetics of the breed in America might have been in trouble, but for a clever woman by the name of Mrs. Pym. She was from Britain but lived in the United States. Being from Britain, she knew what healthy, strong Cardigan Welsh corgis looked like, and so she decided to do something about the poor genetics of the American stock. She went back home and purchased eleven Cardigan Welsh corgis for breeding. Three of these she left behind, but eight came back with her. She traveled by ship across the Atlantic, and it is reported that her fellow passengers were greatly charmed by the eight puppies. While Mrs. Pym bred dogs herself, she also selected breeders across the country, and worked with them, intending to strengthen the genetics of this wonderful breed. If it wasn't for Mrs. Pym, it is unlikely that we would have Cardigan Welsh corgis in North America still today.

Traits and Characteristics of Corgis

Despite the fact that there are still Cardigan Welsh Corgis out there, the two dogs are similar, and you are quite correct in thinking either one to be a corgi. Yet, when most people talk about corgis, they are talking about Pembroke Welsh corgis. Corgis are smart dogs, and they are often very happy and friendly dogs. They will stick by their owners and give them lots of love, but they can also get stuck in their ways if they are trained improperly. But perhaps the clearest sign that a corgi makes a good dog is the fact that the royal family has had more than 30 of them in Queen Elizabeth's lifetime, and it is looking like they won't be leaving the family any time soon.

It should be noted that corgis have very strong personalities and so you should make sure that you are ready to tackle the challenge that a corgi offers. If you are, you've got yourself a great pet, but if not, then you might be setting yourself up for frustration. Many of these are topics that we will be digging into in length, but let us quickly take a look at issues of personality, exercise, diet, training, noise, and relationships. Red flags in this section may be a sign that you aren't ready for a corgi in your life just yet. If so, it may mean you are better off with another breed, or you simply need to take a little bit more time to prepare life and house for a new furball.

While we most often connect larger dogs to their origins in agriculture, hunting, or hauling, many people don't realize that the corgi has roots in this same behavior. That means that just like a bigger dog needs lots of exercise and has a strong work ethic when trained properly, so too do corgis. They might have adorably stubby legs that melt your heart while they run, but they aren't aware of that. Corgis think of themselves as the biggest dogs in the world. While many small breeds have "small dog syndrome" and seem to yap and get overly aggressive to compensate for their size, corgis don't suffer from this trait because they aren't aware they are small.

Corgis are one of the happiest breeds you will find. They love to run and lick and play and bathe and hang out with each other and their humans. If you're looking for a comfort dog, a corgi is pretty much the most joy you can get inside so small of a package. It's hard to feel too lost or sad when you have a corgi trying to cheer you up. Which they will do because they are very responsive. They like to watch what happens in the household, and they have a strong sense of the emotions of their humans. It is wonderful that they are such caring and loving animals that they will take steps to cheer up a sad owner without having to be told.

With that said, it is very important that corgis are trained while they are younger. They are smart dogs, and if you don't take charge and train them early, you probably never will. In fact, you'll likely find that the dog is so stuck in its own behavior and expectations that you feel like you are the one that's been taught. You need to be careful not to get tricked by your corgi. They're adorable and silly and playful, and it is easy to get lost in what they're doing and forget about training until it is too late. But you are going to need to train them well if you are going to be taking them for exercise or socializing them. Keep in mind, though, that as an intelligent breed, corgis need space to make decisions for themselves. They like having a feeling of independence, like being left alone to do their job rather than being told every small detail. A place in your household where the corgi has no demands put on them will help them in this manner.

Given that corgis come from working roots and think of themselves as big dogs, it shouldn't come as a surprise that these little guys need to get a fair deal of exercise. They also have lots of energy to burn through the day. They love being given work to do, like helping with hauling things. Or they'll chase after a ball or a laser pointer. They'll run and play with other dogs and work themselves into a deep sleep. The good news is that, despite all this energy, you can get by on walking them once a day and letting them run twice a week. But you are best off walking them a couple of times a day, letting them run around more often. If you have a yard or a nearby off-leash dog park, then these will make it easier for your corgi to get its exercise.

The previous paragraph mentioned having your corgi help you work. This is actually a better idea than it might sound at first. Since they originate from working dogs, corgis have a strong work ethic themselves. If you can provide them with work they can do to earn treats, then they will strive to do it. This can also include learning new tricks, though you need to start them early enough to get the educational foundation in place for them to properly follow you and learn from you. Keep in mind that, while they want to be involved in family work, they also crave being involved in family play. A corgi isn't like a cat that observes the family. Corgis think of themselves as a member of the family, and they want to be included in everything that is happening around them. They'll feel let down and betrayed if they find out they were left out from something fun. Unfortunately, everything a corgi is left out of is fun in their eyes because that's their one gear, and so you'll be given that betrayed look from time to time. They'll get over it, so long as you show them they're still loved.

Even when started young enough, you are likely to discover that training a corgi is not as quick and easy as it is with other breeds. Corgis are stubborn, independent creatures. But they can learn, so long as you keep at it with patience and love. If you can get the ground floor of training into place, then you can keep teaching a corgi throughout its whole life. When they understand how commands and tricks work, they start to see them as a form of work, and learning new commands results in treats the same way work does. The fastest way to train a dog is through its stomach, and a corgi is no different. It's just going to take a little bit longer than maybe a golden retriever would. They are in no way less capable; they're just more naturally independent, and so they require more reinforcement. You might have heard people, who have failed to train their corgis, call them stupid. The fact is, these are intelligent dogs who probably managed to train their owners instead. If you stick with training, and follow sound methods, you will be able to train your corgi, and you'll see that they are far from being dumb dogs.

Corgis make great watchdogs because that was part of their earliest job, looking out for predators and warning them off. Unfortunately, this can result in a lot of barking. Corgis are also known for taking light bites at the ankles of pets, children, and even adults. They tend to do it to other pets and children more often because they are smaller. These dogs get bored, and their herding instincts start to come out. These bites can be scary to a child or a parent, but they aren't intended to be harmful. They are meant to herd the animal. The dog doesn't realize that these are hurting anyone in any real way. Unfortunately, this doesn't stop them from possibly being dangerous, despite the dog's best intentions. To be a herd animal, they had to protect and care for the herd. This means that they are loyal and protective animals, and so, what they are doing is out of love, and it would likely break their hearts if they knew it was harmful. Some people think a corgi shouldn't be introduced into a family with children under the age of five. This is to make sure any children in the household are old enough to understand what the dog is doing, and so will be less likely to get hurt by the animal. A child who's too young might be hurt more by this, or they may attack the dog and start a fight. Proper training and watchfulness may make this a non-issue, but it is important to understand.

Corgis can be trained not to bark as much, but their natural instinct is to bark at everything and anything. New sounds, new people, new animals, wind noises, car dogs opening, car dogs closing, the neighbors' kids making too much noise, your kids making too much noise, the television. Everything. They bark at everything. Early socialization and training will help to reduce this behavior. It should be a goal to reduce barking rather than eliminate it. Those that teach a dog not to bark through abuse make a dog that is afraid to bark at all. Those that teach a dog to bark less have a dog that isn't afraid to bark it's little head off when a burglar or a dangerous animal starts to threaten the household. A dog that is afraid to bark for fear of punishment may not even bark when the household is on fire. Barking itself is not a bad thing, it is too much barking that is undesirable, and this can be reduced through proper training if started young.

Corgis are also like golden retrievers in that they are a breed that can't be left alone for long periods. A dog that is left alone gets scared and lonely, and it starts to misbehave. More barking, more chewing on furniture and belongings, more scratching, and more indoor accidents happen when a dog is left alone for too long. Considering that corgis are used to being surrounded by cows all the time, it makes sense why they are such social animals. If you have left a corgi alone for a lengthy period, or if it is anxious for other reasons (such as a thunderstorm, perhaps), then you might even find your corgi trying to herd the whole family together because it feels there is safety in numbers. This is a sign that the dog is having a rough time and needs your help. If you can, take a moment to gather with everyone and give the dog some relief. This will comfort the dog, and it can help your family to spend more time together.

Pros and Cons of Having a Corgi

Corgis are very complicated dogs. There are a lot of pros to having a corgi. These little guys have lots to offer, and they are ridiculously easy to love. We're going to take a moment to look at the pros. Afterward, we will be turning our attention to the cons. These will both be weighed with a fair eye to the reality of owning a corgi rather than the sales pitch of a breeder or pet store employee.

The Pros

Corgis are Adorable: Have you ever seen a corgi? They're the cutest thing on this planet, up there with

16

otters and pugs. From their tiny little legs to their big cute smiles and massive energy, having a corgi is an invitation to lots of photos and moments of laughter.

Corgis are Social: They need to be socialized through training when they are young, and if they are, then they get along great with other animals and humans. When they aren't properly trained, they will be more likely to run off another dog or a cat, but, with training, they'll try to become best friends. Plus, they're suckers for scratches and pats, so they make friends with new humans pretty quickly.

Corgis are Smart: People might claim corgis are dumb, but those people have no idea a dog has outwitted them. Corgis are smart, and this can make them hard to teach because they'll want to break you. But, with proper training, this benefits owners massively because they will be able to teach them plenty of tricks. Which brings us to…

Corgis are Hard Workers: Corgis that are taught properly love to work hard and help out their humans. So, it should be no surprise that this makes them a great choice for those that work on farms or do other physical jobs. If you work in the tech world or something else less dog inclusive, then you can always teach them to give you a hand working around the home. They can be trained to fetch items or even call family members to the dinner table. There are an endless number of ways that a corgi could be taught to help you out if you tackle the problem with a little bit of creativity.

Corgis Have Long Lives: If you are nervous about getting a corgi because they don't live long, then you must have heard some internet rumors because these little guys can live up to fifteen years or more. There are more than a few corgis that made it to voting age.

Corgis are Popular: Due in part to the fact that the Royal Family has been raising them, and, in part, to the way they shake their butts when they are excited, corgis have become a popular breed of dog, and people love seeing and sharing photos and videos of them online. If you are concerned about how Insta-worthy your dog is, a corgi is always sure to grab everyone's attention.

The Cons

Corgis are Easily Bored: Corgis are used to being working dogs, and this means that they always knew what they were supposed to be doing. They had a task, and they would give it their attention. They had to run around, keep watch, and make sure nothing happened to the cattle. In the modern age, where corgis are more often house pets, there isn't a whole lot happening. This leaves corgis to get bored when they are neglected or ignored. The result can be destructive or anxious behavior, and it isn't surprising to find a bored corgi trying to herd the household. You need to be able to provide toys, attention, and entertainment to a corgi.

Corgis Shed Like Crazy: Sure, they think that they're big dogs, but we can all see that corgis are quite small. Yet, somehow, they seem to shed and shed and shed as if they were huge. It makes no sense how so much hair can come off such a small dog, but you'd better believe it does. And often. Of course, every dog sheds, but corgis seem determined to do it the most. This can be managed through proper grooming as we'll look at in chapter four, but it will always be something you'll need to put up with.

Corgis Need Lots of Exercise: This is another example where these small dogs get it in their mind that they're big. While they can get away with a daily walk and a couple of times running every week, corgis should be given much more exercise. At least two walks a day and a chance to run every other day would be much more appropriate for a corgi. That's easier to do for people with backyards who can play fetch. But they really should be getting lots of exercise to stay fit and healthy.

Corgis Need Lots of Attention: Corgis can't be left alone for too long, or they start to act up. Even when home with the family, a corgi is going to want attention. That doesn't need to be constant, but addressing the dog to show you remember it is there, and giving it some pets, will go a long way towards keeping it happy. When corgis are ignored, they often resort to herding techniques out of boredom and a feeling of abandonment. If you aren't able to give a corgi enough attention, or you are going to need to leave it alone for long periods of time, then you are better off not getting one.

Corgis are Loud: Corgis are loud, loud dogs. If you properly train a corgi, then you can reduce this. But younger corgis are going to be barking at everything before they are trained. If your corgi ends up training you instead, then you might just have to deal with a dog that barks at everything. If you are concerned about how loud a corgi is, then you are going to have to commit to training.

Corgis Have Dietary Issues: Corgis have a problem with weight. They are one of the easier dogs to overfeed. Again, they are a small dog that thinks they are a big dog, and this includes their stomach. They are also prone to some stomach issues, as we'll be looking at in chapter five, and so, you might not be able to feed a corgi the same food you feed other dogs. This requires a little more money if you have another dog, but, more importantly, it requires attention. You will need to read what is in your corgi's food and be mindful of how much they are eating. That might be a hassle, but reading your pet's food should be a minimum requirement for having any pet.

Corgis are Stubborn: Corgis get set in their ways. We've seen corgis are smart, but this is the reverse of that. Corgis are too smart. You need to commit to training them and work hard at it to come out on top.

Corgis Aren't Great With Kids: If they are trained correctly, then a corgi will be a fine family pet, but they shouldn't be introduced into a family until children are at least five years old. Corgis aren't the easiest dogs in the world to handle, and children can sometimes get frightened or hurt by their behavior.

Pros versus Cons: Results

It should be clear that having a corgi is a lot more work than it seems. They are dogs that need you to pay attention to their exercise, diet, and particularly to their training in a focused way. They can also have issues with being too loud or not fitting in with children. This means that if you are considering bringing one into a family, then you need to educate your children on the dog's behavior, so they'll understand why the dog acts as it does.

However, if you are able to deal with these cons, then the pros can be quite rewarding. Getting a new worker to help you out around the house can be extremely valuable, and these little dogs are very loyal and loving. If you can give them attention and care, then adding one to your life can bring a lot of value.

As with any pet, you should carefully consider what it means to bring them into your home and if you will be able to look after their needs. Corgis are no different, so weigh these pros and cons and compare them before you go ahead.

Chapter Summary

- There are two types of corgi: The Pembroke Welsh and the Cardigan Welsh.

- The Pembroke Welsh corgi has a mysterious history. We aren't sure where they came from, though we have our theories. The mythical origin story is that the Pembroke Welsh corgi was a gift to man from fairies.

- The Cardigan Welsh corgi has been around for more than 3,000 years, and its history is well documented.

- Corgis were originally bred to serve as herd dogs. This has left them with strong herding instincts, despite the fact they're no longer put to such work very often.

- The Pembroke Welsh and Cardigan Welsh corgi are very close to each other. The Cardigan Welsh is more alert, making for efficient watchdogs.

- The Royal Family has taken the Pembroke Welsh corgi as their official breed.

- Corgis are smart dogs, but also very independent. This can make them harder to train, as they often end up controlling their owners instead.

- Corgis think and act like they are bigger dogs than they are. What this means for you as an owner is that they need more food and exercise than other small dog breeds do.

- Corgis are very happy and loving dogs, eager to socialize and hang out with their human friends.

- You need to start training a corgi when they are young. If you wait too long, then you may not be able to train them at all.

- Since their roots are as work dogs, corgis are great helpers and love to be kept busy.

- While they can be trained to reduce the frequency, corgis do bark a lot.

- Corgis can live up to between 15 to 20 years.

- These are smart dogs, which mean they get bored quickly, and this can result in damaged furniture or nipped ankles when they try to herd you.

- Corgis also shed a lot due to their double coats.

- You need to be careful feeding a corgi, as it can be easy to overfeed them. An obese corgi is no joke since their bodies weren't designed for a lot of weight.

- Corgis are also not very great with kids, because of that nipping habit mentioned above. Don't introduce a corgi to a family with children under five.

In the next chapter, you will learn about the minor but noteworthy differences between the Pembroke Welsh corgi and the Cardigan Welsh corgi. While they have a lot in common, these minor differences are important to weigh up before adopting.

CHAPTER TWO

WHICH CORGI SHOULD YOU CHOOSE?

In the last chapter, we looked at the pros and cons of corgis as if they were one dog. In a way, we were acting like the judges that first categorized the dogs in the 1900s. But we've already seen how the Pembroke Welsh and Cardigan Welsh corgis are two different types of dog. The last chapter allowed us to see if we could fit a corgi into our lives in general. This chapter is going to take a moment to help you figure out if the furball you adopt is going to be a Pembroke Welsh or a Cardigan Welsh.

We've already looked at their histories and seen they have a similar background in herding; this is useful because it keeps these two styles close together in terms of personality and temperament. In fact, many people who don't educate themselves before purchasing a corgi, have no idea which one they're raising. We'll consider which of these we're going to bring home before we prepare our living spaces in the next chapter.

Pembroke Welsh Corgis versus Cardigan Welsh Corgis

The differences between these breeds are minor, but there are a few key points that might push you toward one in particular. We'll start with appearance, then personality, and on to health concerns.

If you're one of the people that can tell alligators and crocodiles apart, then you should have no problem spotting the difference between the Pembroke Welsh and the Cardigan Welsh. But if you are like me and most of the world, then you might have a harder time with it since they are both alike in terms of size and color. The biggest difference that people look for between the two is the tail. The Pembroke Welsh corgi has a docked tail, which means a little stubby tail. The Cardigan Welsh corgi, on the other hand, has a full and proper tail. This detail is easy to spot when you know about it, but if you don't, then it is as confusing as the two reptiles I mentioned.

Another way to tell is to look at the feet of the dog. A Cardigan's feet point away from the body, and they are often round. The Pembroke's feet are more oval than the Cardigan's paws, and they point inwards towards the body. This is another one of those details that are minor and hard to tell. The third and last example of this physical difference is in the weight. The Cardigan Welsh Corgi is often heavier than the other, but an overweight Pembroke can throw this determining factor completely out of sync.

We've talked about corgis being friendly and corgis being watchdogs. While either breed can be both, the Pembroke is more naturally friendly, and the Cardigan is more watchful and alert. If you are looking to bring an amiable and loving dog into the family, you will want to go with a Pembroke because they are much better suited for a relaxed and sociable lifestyle. A cardigan isn't necessarily going to be bad in this way, but they are going to want to protect and watch over the household more than they are going to want to meet new people and pets. This doesn't mean that a Cardigan Welsh corgi loves their owners any less; it is just that they show it in a different way. They aren't so much into the pets and kisses; they're more into making sure predators and threats don't disrupt the household. Both of these traits are useful and attractive, but you'll know best which one fits your home environment.

While both Cardigan Welsh and Pembroke Welsh corgis have hereditary diseases and common ailments that need to be dealt with, the Cardigan Welsh Corgi has quite a few less than the Pembroke. Pembroke Welsh Corgis have a tendency to develop epilepsy. They're also vulnerable to disease of the bones. It is possible to adopt a corgi and never encounter health problems, but the chances are lowered depending on the dog's genetics. High-quality breeders will produce healthier puppies than pet stores or adoption centers do. If you are concerned about health problems but want a corgi that will fit into a family, then going with a respectable and well-reviewed breeder can make the difference between a corgi with few medical issues and one with many.

So, while the differences between the Cardigan Welsh corgi and the Pembroke Welsh corgi are quite minor, they can make a large difference. A Cardigan Welsh corgi is not going to be nearly as affectionate and cuddly, but they will make good watchdogs and have fewer health problems overall. Pembroke Welsh corgis are more prone to getting sick, and so it's more advisable to get them from high-quality stock, but they are also more obviously affectionate and fit into families better. Which is right for you will ultimately have to come down to your preferences, but the two are far more similar than they are different.

Chapter Summary

- The differences between the Pembroke Welsh and the Cardigan Welsh corgi are very minor.

- The biggest and easiest difference to spot is their tails. The Pembroke Welsh has a docked tail, while the Cardigan Welsh corgi has a full tail.

- If you look at the feet of a corgi, then you can tell which kind it is since the Cardigan Welsh's feet point away from the body. In contrast, the Pembroke Welsh corgi's feet point inwards.

- The Pembroke Welsh corgi is a very friendly dog, so much so it's likely to try and befriend a burglar. The Cardigan Welsh corgi is more prone to barking, but this also makes them much better watchdogs.

- The Cardigan Welsh corgi also doesn't want to be a part of the family in the same way the Pembroke Welsh does. A Cardigan Welsh corgi will still love the family, but they aren't as cuddly or social.

- The Cardigan Welsh corgi has less hereditary health issues compared to the Pembroke Welsh.

In the next chapter, you will learn how to make your home into the perfect environment for your new corgi. We'll talk about preparing the home for a puppy, the differences between raising a corgi in a house compared to an apartment, and how well these little furballs tolerate being left home alone. Spoiler: Not very well at all.

CHAPTER THREE

THE PERFECT HOME FOR A CORGI

When it comes to adopting any kind of dog, you are going to need to make sure that you can provide a healthy living space that is big enough, interesting enough, and safe enough for a new canine to move into. It doesn't matter if it's a big dog like a golden retriever or a small one like a corgi. Different sizes result in different requirements, but most of these are the same. A dog needs to be able to get around comfortably, after all.

In this chapter, we'll look at exactly what it means to prepare our home for a new corgi inhabitant. The first step is to consider if we have enough space. Some of us live in houses, and these can certainly make for a great home for a corgi, but more and more people live in apartments these days. We'll take a look at what it takes to raise a corgi in an apartment building, so you can figure out if it is worth your time or if you should be looking at another breed to have as your roommate. We'll follow this conversation with a look at how well a corgi can deal with being left alone. They're not very good at it, and so you'll want to be able to fit a corgi into your schedule or get an assist from family, friends, or a dog sitter. We'll finish up the chapter with a look at what steps you should take to prepare your home for a new corgi so that they have what they need and aren't going to get into trouble. With this all understood, you'll be ready to bring your new corgi home and start looking at issues of grooming and health in the following chapters.

Can a Corgi Live in an Apartment?

Everyone loves a corgi; they're such cute dogs that it isn't a surprise they have become one of the internet's favorite creatures. They also seem to be made for the modern lifestyle. People are living in smaller spaces than they used to. Apartments have let us fit a lot of human beings into tight spaces while keeping a moderate level of comfort. A large dog can be hard to fit into an apartment, though there are more than a fair share of owners that have done just that. Thankfully, a smaller breed like a corgi is easier to fit into a small living area.

But does this mean that they take well to apartment living? That question is a bit trickier to answer and will require us to consider the issue from a few different angles to get a full and detailed picture of life with a corgi in an apartment. Corgis have a lot going for them, such as their small size, considerable intelligence, and their highly adaptable nature. Unfortunately, corgis also have a lot of qualities that can make living in an apartment a hard time, such as their noise level, level of excitement, and the non-stop shedding that curses this lovable breed.

Corgis have lots of energy despite their small size. Considering the fact that a corgi can easily sit on your lap, it is shocking just how much energy these little guys have. They can run for a couple of hours at a time. We'll learn more about exercising a corgi in chapter five, but the short of it is that they need plenty of exercise each day, though not in large windows of time. A ten-minute sprint can wipe a corgi's energy out for half a day or more. But as the energy levels start to fill up again, your corgi will begin to get more excited, and they'll want to run around the apartment. We'll be looking at preparing our homes for a corgi in a moment so that they don't manage to get themselves hurt, but this has ramifications when it comes to living in an apartment. If you have neighbors below you, then a hyper-corgi is going to make a lot of noise as they stomp and skitter and prance around. This can be annoying at the best of times, but it can be the most irritating thing in the world for your neighbors if your corgi starts running around too late at night or too early in the morning. If you aren't able to teach your dog to understand it's not allowed to get so active at these times, you'll be faced with constant complaints from people living around you.

Take a moment to consider life for a dog in an apartment. They're full of energy and want to play and run around, but even if they are allowed to, there just isn't enough space for them to do so fully. A corgi that is raised in a house will have more room for running around, and they might even be lucky enough to get a backyard. A corgi with a backyard is going to be able to run and run and run until they're all tuckered out, but not so with an apartment-bound dog. That means that you'll need to stay active with your new dog and take them out for a walk at least once a day. Twice a day would be even better for the corgi's health, and it will help to use up all that energy.

Corgis are bright dogs, and this is great because it means they can adapt to living in an apartment much easier. But corgis aren't only smart; they are also highly social animals. Their intelligence makes it easier for them to learn rules about what they are and aren't allowed to do, as well as make it easier for them to figure out how to get along with the family without getting in the way. The highly social aspect of the corgi is great because it means they won't get bent out of shape by being stuck in a smaller space with some humans. Corgis love their humans, and so this is a plus in the dog's eyes. While corgis can be used as watchdogs, they are more likely to want to meet everyone new who comes over, and so they fit in well in apartments where lots of people are coming and going.

This intelligence can also be a curse since clever dogs are more likely to get bored at a faster rate than a less intelligent breed would. This means that leaving a corgi alone isn't easy to do, as we'll be discussing, but it also means that many of the things that catch your dog's attention will also grow old quickly. A bored corgi can be a hassle since they start to revert to their herding instincts. If you are raising a corgi in an apartment, then there will be less sights, sounds, and spaces for them to explore and discover. The boredom of apartment living can be conquered by investing in a few toys and making sure you never skip one of the dog's walks.

The biggest issue to raising a corgi in an apartment building is the fact that these are very loud dogs. When your corgi is hyper, it isn't their energy that is the problem, but how much noise they make using it up. Corgis are bark-happy dogs who yip and yap at the slightest provocation. This can be massively reduced through early and successful training, but even the best training seldom gets rid of barking in its entirety. Corgis bark when they're happy, when they're bored, when they're surprised, when they hear someone coming home, when they hear neighbors coming home, and for just about every other possible reason you could think of. This is a natural behavior to the dog, which can make for a bad time since punishment needs to be exactly in time to the barks; otherwise, the animal won't know what it did wrong. If you are looking to raise a corgi in an apartment, then barking is going to be the central behavior you need to clamp down on and prepare yourself (and maybe your neighbors) for.

The second biggest issue is shedding. Corgis love to shed. In fact, they are a walking fur coat. Everywhere they go, they leave behind enough dog hair to knit a scarf. This is annoying in a house, but it is even more annoying in a small apartment since the shed hair has nowhere to go, and it all seems to ball up and get over everything. If you have a small apartment, then you will need to prepare yourself for the inevitable fact that you are going to have dog hair all over your couches, chairs, clothes, and sometimes even your food. It can be a major pain that, while some steps can be taken to prevent it, you will need to accept and learn to live with it if you want a corgi.

If you are worried about the noise level of a corgi, then you will want to get one that has already been trained. If you aren't concerned about the noise level, then you can adopt a corgi as a puppy and train them yourself, so long as you remember that these dogs are independent and can be tough for beginners to teach. A corgi can live a perfectly healthy and happy life in an apartment, and they can even be trained to do so without causing issues for the neighbors, but doing so will take time and energy and require you to effort into raising your new canine family member.

Can Corgis Tolerate Being Left Alone?

Leaving a corgi alone is not a good idea. There aren't many dogs that like to be left alone for long periods, but corgis are particularly bad at flying solo. If you're looking to go away for a vacation, you're either going to have to bring the dog with you or hire a dog sitter. Not every corgi is going to have the same psychology, and some corgis may be able to stay alone for longer, while others can't be left alone for more than a couple of hours at most. We'll take a look at what happens when a corgi is left alone, ways you can make it easier for them to handle being on their own for a bit, and we'll even set a time limit on how long our dogs are solitary. If you live an active lifestyle where you're not back at the house very often, then a corgi might not be a good fit for you. Someone that works from home can take their corgi to work with them, or a person with enough friends and family to look after a corgi, can have a fantastic experience raising one of these adorable puppies.

A basset hound or a greyhound can be left alone without any issues, but a corgi is too social an animal for this. They are intelligent too, and this is a horrible combination if you were hoping for a low maintenance pet that can chill out at the house while you're at work. Corgis need lots of social activity in order to stay happy, cheerful, and sane. A corgi that is left on its own may start barking up a storm when they try to reach someone, anyone who will pay attention to them and give them some of that interaction they crave. Another issue is that corgis get bored easily. This is a problem with smart dogs in general, as they don't get lost in their activities the same way a dumber dog does. Even if you are leaving a corgi for only an hour, you should make sure they have plenty of toys at home to keep their attention. Especially useful are toys that require the dog to solve a puzzle to get a treat. The smell of the treat will hold the dog's attention, and this means more time before they start to get bored.

If you leave a corgi at home without anything to keep its attention, then you can almost guarantee that you'll be coming home to find destroyed furniture or possessions. Shoes, remotes, pillows, and chair and table legs are just some of the objects that a corgi might start chewing on to create its entertainment. This behavior can be terribly frustrating to dog owners who weren't expecting to come home to a warzone. But before you get mad at the dog, you need to take into account a couple of factors. First, it is you that brought a corgi into your life, only to leave them at home. Second, you were the one that left the corgi on its own and didn't provide it with enough entertainment. Third, the action that you want to punish the dog for has already come and gone. This means that the corgi will have no idea why you are punishing it. That's particularly bad since it can teach the corgi to be afraid of you coming home. The dog might have destroyed your shoes hours ago, so the only thing the dog understands is that you came back and then got mad at it. So, while it is the happiest animal in the whole world because it gets to see its human friend, you then turn this against the dog and make it a miserable experience. It doesn't address the problem and will only strain your relationship with your corgi.

What's even worse than this is the fact that the destructive behavior of your corgi might be a sign of separation anxiety. Corgis that are left alone often develop this condition. If your dog begins to get upset and nervous every time you get ready to leave, then you might have a corgi with separation anxiety. This is a psychological problem that will leave your corgi feeling miserable. If you are mindful of not leaving them alone too much, then you are unlikely to see separation anxiety develop, but when it does, it can be mistaken for a sign that your dog is bored. If you come home to a lot of destruction, then you should first get the dog some more toys to keep it stimulated while you are away. If this gets rid of the destructive behavior, then boredom was the issue. If the toys do nothing and you still come home to destroyed property or messy accidents around the house, then the chances are good you are dealing with separation anxiety and should consult a vet about how to best train, teach, and treat the dog.

With these factors in mind, we can set ourselves a good time frame for how long to leave a corgi alone. Our first consideration needs to be the age of the corgi. A puppy can't be left alone nearly as long as a full-grown dog can. How long a puppy can be left alone depends on its age, as a puppy has much smaller bowels than a grown dog. If your puppy is two months old, then they can be left alone for three hours. Three months old can be left alone for four hours, and so on. However, you shouldn't leave a puppy alone the full length of time just because you can. A puppy needs much more stimulation, and so you shouldn't leave a puppy alone for more than two to three hours at the most. A full-grown corgi, on the other hand, can be left alone much longer, but you shouldn't leave your corgi alone for more than six hours. That will ensure you are home in time to let the dog out before it has an accident, but it also lets you socialize, bond, and interact with your corgi, all things that it needs and wants.

You don't need to physically come back home to your corgi within six hours so long as somebody can. If you live with your partner or family, then this can be a lot easier to figure out and schedule. But if you live alone, then you will need to carefully consider whether or not you can make it home often enough to take care of the dog. Getting someone to look after your corgi is one way of making the experience easier, but it might also cost money and can quickly cost you a pretty penny if you need to pay for a dog sitter every day.

If you can get home often enough to check in on your corgi, then they can do just fine on their own, but the real issue is when they're left for extended stretches at a time. If you work six-hour shifts, your corgi should be able to adapt to you being gone at set times, but switching up that schedule will also cause the dog lots of discomfort and confusion. If you need to be gone longer than normal, you should hire or ask someone to stop in and see your corgi, so that they aren't left feeling scared and abandoned.

Preparing Your Home for a Corgi Puppy

If you have double-checked your scheduling and are sure you can provide a comfortable home to your corgi, then the last step before adopting is to take a few minutes and prepare the household itself. You want to remove things that the dog could break or get into, plus work out a new schedule for your corgi, and get all the food, snacks, and toys necessary to keep your corgi entertained and healthy. While there is no real order to the steps that follow, you should have them done before bringing the corgi into your home.

Let's begin with the shopping. If you are looking to bring a corgi into your household, you need to have all the tools necessary for taking care of them. You'll want to get a collar and a leash so you can take them for walks. Food and water dishes are top priorities. While a dog will have no problem eating off the floor, teaching them that a bowl is theirs and to expect food in it will lead to a cleaner life. Make sure to get both soft and hard food, as the best diets use a combination of both. Grooming is important, so make sure to get doggy brushes, shampoo, and conditioner. Lots of toys are going to be necessary, especially if you are bringing a corgi puppy home and not a fully-grown dog. You'll need a kennel to pick up the dog or take them to the vet. A dog bed is a must with a corgi, as they need to have a space they consider theirs. You may also want to get treats and basic medical supplies. Your corgi puppy will be growing a lot, so you may want to invest in larger and bigger toys ahead of time so that there is always something just right for the dog.

Next, consider your household itself and whether or not it is ready for a puppy. Are there valuables that could be easily knocked over? What about exposed power cords that a puppy might want to chew? If you have plants around the house, do you know if they are dangerous to a corgi? Are the plant pots going to be a digging temptation? Do you have any food storage that the puppy could get into? If so, you will want to move it to a more secure location. Once you have gone through the house and made sure that nothing will hurt your puppy, go through again and make sure there aren't any small objects that a puppy could eat or choke on. You'll want to sweep and vacuum thoroughly prior to bringing a puppy home.

Creating a schedule beforehand is always smart. Dogs are creatures of habit, and so they learn your schedule, and they use this to establish their internal clocks and understanding of reality. Puppies need lots of extra work, too, and so setting a schedule will make it simpler to ensure everything gets done on time. Plan out your walks, feeding, bathroom breaks, and surprises. Puppies need to eat up to four times each day, and then they'll need to go to the washroom afterward. Plan out a schedule and put a checkmark next to each item as you hit it. As you and your puppy bond and get more comfortable with each other, you'll find that both you and the corgi don't need the schedule as much. But when a corgi is new and isn't sure what's happening, a schedule helps to give some balance and consistency to life, and this can make the move from one location to a scary new home much easier.

Finally, regardless of the fact that you prepared your house for the corgi, you will still find there are some problems that you'll need to tackle and deal with. Puppies want to chew on everything, and this is going to happen no matter how hard you try to prevent it. Something you care about is going to get wrecked, it just always seems to work this way. Remember that your corgi doesn't mean you any harm, and they would be heartbroken to learn they broke something you enjoyed. They are loving animals, but they are still animals and young ones at that. They need to be given time and patience to grow and adapt to their new family, home, and lifestyle. When you offer this patience and understanding, you will find that training and integrating a new corgi into your life was a lot of work, but absolutely worth every second of it.

Chapter Summary

- With modern lifestyles as they are, more and more people are raising dogs in apartments. Thankfully, a corgi can adapt to an apartment life if it needs to.

- Corgis are quite small, and so they can easily fit into an apartment.

- These dogs have lots of energy, and they are bark-happy. Both of these behaviors can cause a lot of issues when living in an apartment.

- Since corgis need lots of energy, you will need to take them outside more often when you live in an apartment. They feel cooped-up and need to let loose.

- Corgis are social animals and love their humans with all their hearts, and so they don't mind the small quarters so long as they can hang out with you.

- Apartments don't usually offer much to smell, hear, or watch. This results in a more easily bored dog, and this can lead to damaged property.

- These little dogs shed a lot, and this can make a small apartment super messy in no time at all.

- If you are worried about whether or not a corgi puppy can be trained for your apartment, then you are better off going with a different breed or getting a corgi that has already been trained.

- Corgis don't take well to being left alone. They can develop separation anxiety.

- A bored corgi will destroy furniture when left alone, but so will one that has separation anxiety. Provide your corgi with plenty of toys. If the destructive behavior remains, it is likely due to anxiety.

- An excellent toy for a corgi alone at home is a treat puzzle that requires them to solve minor challenges to earn a hidden reward.

- A corgi should not be left alone for more than six hours. Puppies can only be left alone for a couple of hours since their small bowels can only hold on for so long.

- Corgis require lots of attention, and so you will want to recruit a friend or family member to check up on them if you are going to be out for too long.

- Prepare to adopt a corgi by first getting bowls, toys, and any other supplies you need.

- Go through your house and hide anything that the puppy can break or get into. Anything that will make them sick should be stored well out of their range.

- Create a schedule prior to adopting the puppy so that you know exactly when you are feeding, walking, and training them. Sticking to a timetable will make it easier for the corgi to adapt to its new home.

- Remember that no matter how well you prepare your house, a corgi puppy will find a way to get into something they're not supposed to. Just make sure it isn't anything dangerous. Be prepared to have a remote, shoe, or something else chewed on past the point of fixing.

In the next chapter, you will learn everything you need to know about grooming your corgi. We'll look at how to properly brush and maintain their fur coat before we move on to how to bathe these playful fluffs. We'll also take a look at how to trim their coats before moving on to the issue of shedding to see how much hair they lose, and how you can make it easier to clean up.

CHAPTER FOUR

GROOMING YOUR CORGI

Preparing your home for a corgi isn't the end of the preparations you need to make to look after one of these cutie pies. Issues such as diet, exercise, and training are all significant aspects you are going to need to learn if you want to raise a corgi that is healthy and happy. But there is one section of corgi care that is often overlooked by new owners: grooming.

Grooming is a core part of taking care of any dog, let alone a corgi. Despite their small size, corgis can get into lots of messes. In fact, their tiny size may make it easier for a corgi to get dirty when compared to another breed like the short-haired greyhound. A corgi's coat of fur is considered to be within the same category as the greyhound's, but a corgi's short stature puts them closer to the ground and makes it easier for them to get covered in dust, dirt, or mud. Mud is going to need to be washed off; dust and dirt, on the other hand, can be brushed off.

In this chapter, we'll cover these vital steps to grooming your corgi. We'll begin with brushing to learn the best brushes and tricks for ensuring a clean corgi. From there, we'll move onto bathing, which is much more straightforward with a small dog like a corgi than it is with a golden retriever or greyhound. Corgis will need to have their fur trimmed from time to time, but it is extremely important that we know how to do this the right way, or we can damage the corgi's double coat of fur. We'll cover how to properly trim a corgi before moving on to the tips to reduce the frustration of shedding.

Brushing a Corgi

When it comes to our corgis, we want them to be soft, fluffy, and adorable. This comes quite naturally to a corgi, but they are going to need an assist from you if they are to maintain proper hygiene. Big messes are going to require a bath, but these can be done sparingly. Our best way of helping out our fluffy corgi buddies is to brush their fur every single day. There are at least four reasons for grooming your corgi that immediately pop to mind. Brushing removes dirt and other grime. It also is used to work out tangles in the fur, which is less of a proper for corgis than longer haired dogs, but it is still common enough to be worth noting. A daily grooming habit will let you bond with your corgi as you spend time together, and some of the brushes will be very soothing for your dog. Not every brush is enjoyable, however, and so it is useful to understand the purpose of each and use the more uncomfortable brushes in shorter bursts. However, these uncomfortable brushes are important because they help to reduce the spread of sheddings. With all these benefits, you absolutely must brush your corgi.

Before we get into the brushes themselves, we should take a moment to consider how a corgi's fur is laid out, as this will have a direct impact on what brushes we need. Many dogs have what is called a double coat. Looking at your corgi, what you see right away is called the top coat. This is the hair that sticks out, and it has the feeling and texture of what we call fur. Underneath this top layer is the inner layer. This layer has a different feeling than the top layer, almost more like a short beard than a coat of fur. Between the two coats is enough empty space. Having a double coat is great for a dog because it helps to resist water and dries off faster, but even more important is the fact that a double coat traps air between the two layers. During the winter, this air heats up to help keep your corgi warm, while during summer, the air acts like a personal air conditioner to keep the dog's temperature down. This double coat requires extra steps be taken when grooming and trimming the dog, though this isn't unique to the corgi as a breed.

Corgis are unique in the way they shed. Many dogs with a double coat shed twice a year. For example, the golden retriever sheds their summer coat to prepare for winter, and they shed their winter coat to prepare for summer. Of course, this doesn't take into account the shedding of the puppy coat, but this only happens once in a lifetime. While a golden retriever's two shedding periods a year still leaves shedding as an annoyance to be dealt with, it seems like heaven compared to what happens with a corgi. Corgis don't just shed twice a year; they lose hair the whole year round. This makes taking care of a corgi a more time-consuming experience, but even more important is the value it adds to brushing. Brushing doesn't just make a corgi look good; it also helps them to shed properly and in a healthy manner.

Plus, brushing lets you gather up that excess hair for easy disposal rather than having to wait until it is all over the sofa. Since corgis have more than one coat of fur and they have a variety of grooming needs, it is important to provide them with the right types of brushes.

To best look after a corgi, we will require three brushes. The first is a bristle brush. When it comes to most dogs, we either purchase a bristle brush or a pin brush. Breeds with heavier fur can use these two brushes interchangeably. If you already have a pin brush, then it isn't going to hurt your corgi, but it also isn't going to be as effective as a bristle brush. Bristle brushes should be considered as your most basic brush. It isn't going to help with shedding, and it isn't even going to help with getting at the bottom coat. A bristle brush is made up of lots of tiny bristles that separate the corgi's hair and dislodge any dirt that has become trapped in it. You can use a bristle brush on a corgi multiple times a day since it won't hurt the dog. Using a bristle brush on your corgi is the equivalent of running a comb through your own hair. It doesn't hurt, and while it doesn't do a lot of deep cleaning, it knocks loose fuzz and dirt and leaves the hair looking maintained and beautiful.

Another important brush is what is called an undercoat rake. Sometimes simply referred to as a rake, these are good tools for helping you to deal with shedding. A rake is made up of a row of prongs that easily push aside the coarse hair from the top coat so that they can get at the hair of the bottom coat. The prongs catch onto hairs and help pull them out. This is important because your corgi can use assistance to shed properly. If a hair doesn't fully come out like it is supposed to, then that can cause medical issues and discomfort. An undercoat rake will help to pull free these loose hairs and prevent them from causing any problems down the road. The only issue is that an undercoat rake is not a very enjoyable experience. You need to be extremely careful when using one. Start by purchasing an undercoat brush that has prongs of roughly the same length as the corgi's hair. This will make it harder for the prongs to push into the skin or cause any harm there. Next, be very careful when using it and avoid applying too much pressure. You only need to do one or two passes on a corgi at a time with an undercoat rake, though regular brushing with an undercoat rake is necessary for the corgi's health and in reducing the spread of shed.

Finally, we can use a slicker brush to top off the grooming. A slicker brush is like a mixture of the bristle brush with the undercoat rake. A slicker brush uses small pieces of metal like the bristle brush does, but they are much stiffer on a slicker brush. The ends of each bristle also have a distinct curve that helps them to catch onto undercoat hairs that are ready to be tugged loose. A slicker brush can be used in combination with an undercoat rake; in fact, it is most effective when used in combination. However, many owners seem to think that you need either an undercoat brush or a slicker brush and so they only purchase one. Worse yet, are those who think that a slicker brush works as a replacement for a bristle brush. They might be close in appearance, but a bristle brush is a calming experience free of discomfort. The bristle brush primarily cleans the outer layer. A slicker brush looks similar, but it pushes through the outer layer to focus on tending to the inner layer. You may be able to get away with using a slicker brush without an undercoat rake, but you should never use an undercoat brush to clean the outer coat. It would be like trying to cut a pizza with a spoon: there is a right tool for the job and a wrong tool, and it is vital we know which is which if we want to keep our corgis groomed and gorgeous.

Now that we know which brushes we are using, we need to take a moment to consider how we should be using them. Obviously, we need to run the brushes through our corgi's fur, but there is more to brushing your canine pal than this. How often we brush our corgi, what order we use the brushes, how long we use them, and how rough we are doing it, will all make a notable difference in the outcome of the grooming session. If you want your corgi to enjoy grooming and look great, then the following tips are necessary to create an experience that is enjoyable for both the dog and yourself.

We've mentioned it briefly above, but it deserves going over once again: be gentle when grooming your corgi. Have you ever brushed your hair in a hurry to get out the door and noticed it hurt to pull through tangles? We understand why this is and that we didn't mean any harm to ourselves. But a corgi can't understand this experience. They don't know what brushing is, after all. From the corgi's perspective, their owner has brought them over to play with their hair. This can be a lot of fun; in fact, it *should* be a lot of fun. But we need to be careful about the pressure we use on our little guys. We might be in a rush and want to get the job done, or we might not be thinking about it sufficiently, and we use too much force. Regardless of the reason, the result is the same: a hurt corgi. While this pain will mostly cause irritation, causing any discomfort to our dogs is going to be a miserable experience for us. But it is even more miserable to the dog since they don't understand why you're hurting them. Always brush gently and go over the coat a couple of times rather than try to get it in one rushed and hurried pass.

Next, you should be brushing your corgi on a daily basis. Honestly, you should be brushing any dog on a daily basis, but most of them only need to have their outercoat taken care of. But a corgi sheds all year round. That means they are at risk of developing issues with their coat at any time of the year. You can make this easier by brushing your corgi once or even twice a day. This also helps to turn brushing into a routine that the corgi is used to and even grows to look forward to. This is great for reducing the spread of shed, as well as giving you another chance to bond with your corgi pal. But there is another benefit to creating a daily habit of grooming. Your corgi might not understand that you didn't mean to hurt them when you're using an undercoat rake on their fur. This can result in a moody, distant dog. But if you have a daily routine, then your dog is going to be far more likely to realize that the pain is outside of the normal experience. You may still have a dog that is hurt or irritated, but it is far less likely to treat you like this was an intentional action on your part.

Part of grooming your corgi is to leave them looking gorgeous. If this is a concern of yours, then you are going to want to use your brushes in a specific order. Begin with the undercoat rake or the slicker brush. These push under the outer layer to take care of the undercoat. That means that these brushes aren't concerned with the way that they leave the dog looking. Often fur will be sticking out and looking silly after use with one of these brushes. The secret is to start with these, and then move to the bristle brush as the last step in the process. Many owners will reach for the bristle brush first since it is the easiest to use, and they'll give the dog a quick once-over. If this is all you are doing, then the bristle brush is fine. But if you are doing a full brushing, then you will want to save the bristle brush for last so that it can smooth over the outer coat, putting everything back where it belongs and leaving it looking sleek and well maintained.

In this way, we start from the core of the dog (the tightest coat) and work our way out. This helps to get dirt and grime out from the undercoat. If we started with the bristle brush, then this grime can end up trapped in the overcoat or the layer between the two coats. Using the bristle brush last will make sure this dirt is knocked free from the dog rather than left to decay and attract more grime.

The final tip for grooming your corgi is to make sure that you are brushing them enough. The internet seems to be divided on this particular issue. Some owners say to only give the dog a quick brushing. Others say to brush and brush until there are no more loose hairs coming off. If this were the case, then you'd end up with a naked corgi long before the hair stopped coming out. Instead, brush your corgi for ten to fifteen minutes. If you have three brushes, allocate five minutes to each one. If you only have a brush for the undercoat and one for the overcoat, then give each brush five to seven minutes each. This will make sure that the corgi gets a thorough brushing without keeping them under the brush so long that it becomes an irritation. If you are brushing your corgi twice a day, then use the lower end of these numbers and use the higher end if you are only brushing once a day. If you follow this advice, then you'll have a gorgeous looking corgi with a well-maintained coat of shiny, beautiful fur.

Bathing a Corgi

Bathing your dog is an important part of owning a corgi. These little guys are close to the ground, and they're packed full of energy. That means they're going to run around and get as dirty as can be if they are allowed. Dirt and dust are removed and cleaned away by a solid brushing. Mud and stickier messes are going to require a bath; otherwise, you'll have a corgi tracking mud throughout the house. This is a common experience since their low bodies leave them at the perfect level to soak up lots of sticky stuff. Still, dogs don't need to be washed nearly as often as we humans do. We'll cover when to wash your corgi, how to wash them, and how to make the experience easier through a few tips and tricks.

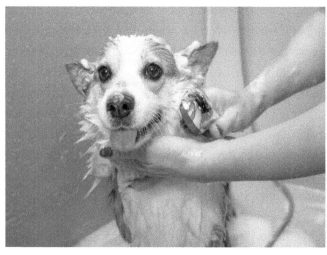

You are going to need to purchase some supplies before you can bath your corgi. If you are bathing inside, then you will want a towel, a blowdryer, some petroleum jelly, a cup/bowl/pot to scoop water with, and any shampoo or conditioner that you'll be using on the puppy's fur. You can also bath a corgi outdoors if you like. You shouldn't bathe a dog outside if it is cold out, but otherwise, all you need is a plastic tub for the corgi to sit in while you wash it.

Getting your corgi into the bath might prove to be tougher than you'd think. Lots of dogs enjoy their baths, but just as many seem to be put off by the experience. If you told them to hop into a pond, there would be no delay, but something about the artificial nature of the bathtub can really bother some dogs. If this is the case, then you may benefit from bathing outside rather than indoors, as the natural environment is more in tune with the dog's instincts. It can also be a good idea to get a friend or family member to give you a hand. If you have a dog that is put off by the experience, then having an extra set of hands is almost a must. Get your partner to keep the dog from leaving the tub, and they can also offer treats and calming words to help settle them down. If you start bathing your puppy at an early age, then the chances are good that they'll learn to enjoy the bath, and you won't have any problems. But when you are first starting out, it can be quite difficult to get your corgi to stay still.

One of the reasons that bathing a corgi can be so awkward is the fact that it isn't done very often. We brush our corgis every day, and so they get used to this behavior quickly. But when it comes to bathing, we don't have this option. We could technically bath them every day if we wanted, but doing so would damage their fur since it would stop healthy oils from working through the coat. These oils are necessary for your corgi to have that healthy shine. Without them, their fur will begin to look dead and frail. That would defeat the purpose of grooming a corgi in the first place, so let's do our best to avoid overwashing them. That leaves us with the question of how often is often enough when it comes to bathing a corgi?

There are two different answers to this question. They may seem to contradict each other, but they are both correct. The first answer is that you should wash your corgi every 45 days or once every month and a half. This is the baseline level for bathing your dog. If you have a corgi that isn't very active, then the chances are good that they can get away with being bathed once every two or two and a half months. Use the activity level of the corgi to help set whether you should bath them every 45 days or every 60 days.

The second answer is that a corgi should be bathed whenever necessary. That may seem to contradict the first answer because it can result in much earlier and closer-together washes. If you take your corgi out to go tramp through the mud, then you are going to want to wash them afterward. You may settle for a spray down, but gunk like mud should really receive a full wash. If your corgi goes for a swim, then you may want to give them a wash as well, though a splash with the garden hose may be enough to get the job done and clean the dog off. Set a schedule to wash the dog every 45 days or so, and wash them as necessary in between. If you wash your dog on a scheduled day, only to have them get caked in mud a couple of days later, then you'll want to wash off the muddy dog regardless of how close it was to the last bath. This is because these washings represent "emergencies." They're not medical emergencies, but they are cleaning emergencies. Just make sure that if you need to bathe your corgi suddenly, you adjust the next scheduled bath to be 45 days after the new one rather than the previously planned one.

To bathe your dog, fill up the tub with warm water. You want to make sure the water temperature isn't too cold or too hot, but just right for your puppy so that they aren't uncomfortable. Take a moment and get the water temperature right before you introduce the dog to the bath. This way, you avoid accidentally causing discomfort or pain. That's especially important if you are bathing them outside since the sitting water from a garden hose gets to be very hot and can easily hurt your corgi. Once the water is the right temperature, put the dog into the tub and start massaging it.

You'll want to use circular motions to run your fingers through the dog's fur. If we just pour water on our corgi, then the outer coat is going to get wet, but the inner layer will mostly stay dry. We want to use our fingers throughout the corgi's fur so that we entirely soak the undercoat. You can start to work in shampoo once both of your corgi's coats are soaked. Use the same circular motions to work the shampoo throughout both coats. Once the dog is properly shampooed, use the scooping tool you grabbed to rinse the dog off. You may also use a hose or a showerhead; just make sure you are mindful of the pressure on the dog's skin and avoid spraying towards their face. Once the shampoo is rinsed out, you can repeat these steps with the conditioner.

Your corgi is going to be soaking wet when they come out of the bath. The first thing that they are going to want to do is shake all of the water off of themselves like a cartoon dog does. This isn't a problem outside, but if you are bathing them indoors, then you won't want this water splashing everywhere. Take the towel and stretch it over and around your corgi while giving them enough room to move and shake. The towel will catch most of the water, and then you can wrap up the corgi to help towel them off. Toweling a dog will only get rid of so much water, though it is more effective on a small dog than, say, a golden retriever or other long-haired canines. If you want to speed up the drying process, then a hairdryer can be a help. Remember that the air is very hot, and your corgi has no way of telling you when it is starting to burn. Make sure you hold the blow dryer away from the dog rather than too close.

If you want to make bathing your corgi easier, then there are one or two tricks you can use. First off, treats can make an apprehensive corgi much more willing to get into a bath. A toy can also help to keep their attention during this time; just make sure that you select a shampoo and conditioner that aren't harmful when ingested since the toy is likely to get covered in soapy water. The biggest secret of all, the trick that can make the difference between a happy corgi and an uncomfortable one, is the petroleum jelly. Stick your finger in the petroleum jelly and apply a little bit around the eyes, ears, and nose of the dog. Doing that will make it more difficult for water to get into these vulnerable areas, and it helps to prevent infection and discomfort. If you follow these steps, then you'll have a squeaky clean corgi in no time.

Trimming a Corgi

Trimming your corgi is one of those activities which can easily lead to lots and lots of problems if you aren't careful. We talked earlier about how corgis have a double coat. This means that they have an outer layer that helps to fight off water, dust, grime, and germs. This outer coat is also responsible for creating the pocket between the inner and outer coats so that the corgi's fur traps air and creates a natural air conditioning effect. The fact that your corgi has a double coat is one of the reasons that it sheds so much, but it also complicates the act of trimming.

You will need to learn about the difference between these two coats. If I am going to cut my hair, then I just take some scissors and can snip off anything that bothers me. But if I am going to be trimming my corgi, then I need to be extremely careful of where and what I cut. The double coat only maintains its air conditioning effect so long as everything is in place. When you trim a corgi, you cut only one of the coats at a time. Trimming in this manner will leave everything working like it usually should for your corgi. But if you cut through both layers at the same time, then you rupture the air conditioning process by effectively puncturing the "tube" that the air traveled through. Instead of spreading evenly all the way around the dog, it now has a location to vent out and thus ruins the effect as a whole. So while the double coat is responsible for the corgi's issue with shedding, it is also necessary for making sure that your dog can regulate and maintain the right temperature. If you mess this up, then they will be too cold in winter and too hot in the summer, and this will be harmful to their sense of wellbeing.

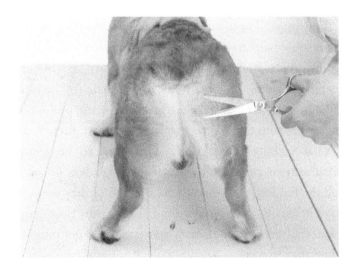

69

Rather than setting a schedule for trimming your corgi, you should trim the dog only when it becomes noticeable that it needs attention. Begin the trim by reaching for the combs first, not the scissors. You'll want either the bristle brush or a comb for human hair. As you comb your corgi, you want to separate the different pieces of hair. Run the comb down the side of the leg, then the back of the leg, the other side, and finally the front. As you separate and get everything straightened out, you will have a much easier time of seeing what needs a quick trim and what doesn't. Begin from the back and work your way forward, making sure not to forget about the paws.

The first thing you'll want to trim away is any matted fur. Any dog with long enough hair is prone to getting mats. These are just tangles of fur that can be impossibly hard to get rid of. Your first line of defense against mats is regular brushing sessions. If you are keeping these up on a daily basis, then mats will be rare. Take the matted hair in one hand, and gently pull it out and away from the dog so that when you cut, there is no risk of nicking doggy flesh. You need to be gentle because mats often pull a lot of the dog's hair at once, and the harder you pull at them, the tighter they seem to go. This is also why you should always trim your corgi when they are dry since mats tighten up and get tougher when they're wet.

When you trim the dog's fur, only start with a quarter of an inch. If you take off too much fur, then there is nothing that you can do to fix the problem. But if you take off too little, you can always even it up and make it neat and level. Mats don't count in this formula as they are their own thing. Start by first looking for any places in which the fur puffs out and is longer than the hairs around it. Cut these to even up the coat and keep it looking uniform. Next, trim the long hairs of the tail, starting from the base of the tail and working down towards the tip. From there, you can begin to work your way from the back of the dog to the front, carefully removing only those hairs that are sticking out. Continue this until you finish with all four legs, the tail, the torso, and the dog's neck.

Make sure you don't forget the paws. Paws need the most trimming between the toes and around the pads of the feet. Hairs grow too long and start to stick out and up from between toes. These are uncomfortable for a dog and can result in a clumsier animal. Removing these will help them to have better control over their motor functions. You may want to trim the dog's nails while you are looking after their feet.

The final step is to finish up with the corgi's head. You need to be extremely careful here, and it is a smart idea to switch to a pair of safety scissors, something that won't blind the dog if they suddenly twist and turn in your hands. Trimming around the face can be tough to pull off if you have a nervous dog, so some owners wait until their corgi is sleeping before making these trims. Once the dog is asleep, simply lift an ear to trim the hairs here, and then carefully remove any hairs around the eyes or face that is unwieldy. With the face done, you now have a freshly trimmed corgi on your hands.

The Ins and Outs of Corgi Shedding

It's been mentioned before, and it will likely be mentioned again, but corgis are heavy shedders. *The Smart Canine* did a survey in which they asked ten different corgi owners about how much their dogs shed. These ten users were experienced with more than fifteen different corgis. Responses ranged from extreme shedding to moderate shedding, but every single user mentioned shedding as an issue to deal with. In ten replies, 60% claimed their corgis were heavy shedders. What this tells you is that, at best, you can expect medium shedding but that you are better prepared if you expect the worst.

Corgis lose hair for a few reasons. One key moment for a corgi is when they say goodbye to their puppy fur. Puppies have a single-layer fur coat that they need to shed to grow in their double coat. So this singular, early shedding period, is in a way responsible for all the shedding that comes after since it is this double coat that results in the most hair loss. Dogs with double coats lose far more than those with single coats. They have twice as much fur to lose, after all. Keep in mind, though, that this extra shedding isn't unique to corgis but shared with most double-coated dogs.

Also in common with most dogs, is the twice-yearly shedding season. During fall and the spring, corgis enter into a period where they lose even more hair than normal. That's because they need to get rid of their winter or summer coats. This is another cycle that is typical with almost every breed of dog. Another element that corgis share with other dogs is the fact that sometimes shedding can be a sign that there is something wrong with the animal's health. We'll be looking at this more in the next chapter, but if your corgi isn't getting the proper nutrients, then they are likely to shed hair as a response. Yet another trigger is stress. We joke that stress makes us want to pull our hair out, but for dogs, this can actually be true. A dog may shed because it is stressed, or it may lick itself as a way of dealing with stress, and this excessive licking can lead to further hair loss. If your corgi is shedding due to stress, then you will need to address the issue that is causing the anxiety in the first place; otherwise, all of the shedding techniques we cover won't make a lick of difference. But if your dog is shedding normally, then these following tips will help make your life a little less hairy.

To begin with, you should be brushing your corgi on a daily basis. In fact, a twice-daily basis is even better.

Not only does this promote clean fur and doggy bonding time, but it also helps remove hairs. Many people brush their corgis and find more hair than they thought their corgi could have. Collecting the fur by brushing will help you to remove a ton of hair that would have just fallen off and covered everything otherwise. After brushing, your best bet is to reduce the stress in the dog's life and make sure it is getting enough nutrients in its diet.

Brushing is the number one way we have to deal with corgi shedding. The other tricks that owners use aren't to deal with the shedding, but to deal with the hair itself. It can be a smart idea to use sheets over the furniture during the fall and spring. These can get covered in corgi hair as much as they like; all you need to do to clean them is take them off and toss them in the wash. You should also find the money to purchase a small vacuum. You want one that creates a tight seal around the hose while being flexible enough to run over the couch and get into the cracks between the cushions. These methods might be reactionary instead of proactive, but they are the best options we have when it comes to shedding corgis.

Chapter Summary

- Grooming a corgi will help to keep them looking beautiful, as well as keep them healthy.

- Corgis are quite low to the ground, and this results in them getting dirty. The best bet for cleaning off dirt and grime is to brush your corgi every day. If you can afford the time and energy to brush your corgi twice daily, then this is even better. No need to go up to three.

- A corgi has a double coat. That means they have an outer and an inner coat. These two layers work together to protect the dog from germs and water, as it is harder for these elements to pass through the outer coat. The two coats also work to trap air between them to warm the corgi up in the winter and cool them off in the summer.

- The corgi's double coat leaves them shedding all year round, not just during the spring and fall when they are preparing for their new coats.

- Because a corgi has such complicated fur, we need to use a few different brushes to groom them.

- A bristle brush is used to knock dirt free from the outer coat, and to keep the hair looking beautiful and straight.

- An undercoat rake is used to brush the undercoat, and to help it to shed properly.

- A slicker brush is like a combination of the bristle brush and undercoat rake, though it should be used along with the undercoat rake rather than replace it.

- We should be mindful to be gentle when we brush our corgi. Bristle brushes aren't going to be a problem, but undercoat and slicker brushes can cause a lot of discomfort if they aren't used carefully.

- Always start with the undercoat, and then finish up a grooming session with the bristle brush.

- Corgis should be bathed once every month and a half or whenever they get really dirty.

- A doggie bath should use warm water, never hot or cold. Always get the water temperature set before introducing the dog to the water.

- Some dogs really don't like the tub. Some of them don't seem to mind it so long as it is outside, while others will require you to get a partner to help make the process easier.

- Put petroleum jelly around the ears, nose, and eyes of the corgi so that water and shampoo don't get in.

- Massage your fingers through the corgi's fur until the undercoat is entirely soaked. Then repeat this with shampoo. Rinse the shampoo off and repeat with your conditioner.

- Hold up a towel so your corgi can shake themselves off without getting water everywhere. Wrap them in a towel or use a blowdryer to help them finish drying off.

- When you trim a corgi, only trim one layer of their fur at a time. If you trim both the inner and outer coat, this will destroy their ability to regulate their body temperature.

- Never trim a wet dog, as this makes it much more difficult, and also makes mats harder to cut.

- Start by carefully snipping away any mats in the dog's fur. Then work down each leg, followed by the paws and the tail. Work your way up the body to the neck.

- The area around the eyes and ears of a corgi will need to be trimmed from time to time. Use blunt scissors to avoid injury. You may want to wait until the corgi is sleeping, so you can trim these sensitive areas while they are calm.

- Only trim away a quarter of an inch at a time. You can always trim more, but you can never put fur back onto the dog.

- Corgis shed their puppy coat, as well as twice a year in the fall and the spring. Yet they also just seem to shed non-stop the whole year anyway.

- Brushing your corgi every day will help to reduce the amount of shedded hair you find in your meals.

- You may want to put sheets over your furniture during the heavy shedding months, as these are easy to remove and clean.

In the next chapter, you will learn how to keep your corgi healthy. To this end, we will start by looking at their lifespans to see how many years we have with these cuties. From there, we'll move onto common ailments like infections and allergies, as well as how to spot and treat them. This moves into the hereditary diseases which plague these lovely animals, as well as how much exercise they need and what makes for a healthy diet.

CHAPTER FIVE

HOW TO KEEP YOUR CORGI HEALTHY

If you are going to be bringing a new canine into your family, then it is necessary to realize the health issues that they may face as they get older. Corgis are prone to many different problems that can reduce their comfort or even cause death. By understanding these diseases and ailments, we can spot the early warning signs and get our corgis treatment quickly.

In this chapter, we cover corgi health in all its ups and downs. We'll take a look at their lifespans, the common ailments that trouble them, and the hereditary diseases which plague them. From there, we'll move into exercising and dieting so that our corgis are kept in the best possible shape. When a corgi is fit and fed, they are much more resilient to ailments like those found throughout this chapter.

The Lifespan of a Corgi

Corgis live for a reasonably long time when compared with most dogs. We've seen that there are Cardigan Welsh corgis and Pembroke Welsh corgis, but this difference is negligible when it comes to lifespan. Both types of corgi live to a median age of 12. Of course, a median age means that there are those much lower but also those much higher. The oldest corgi on record lived to be 29, so there is a chance that you can share much more than 12 years with your corgi. Let's take a look at what factors affect a corgi's projected lifespan.

It is a known fact that large animals live much longer than smaller ones, but this fact is flipped on its head when it comes to dogs. Rather than larger dogs living longer, it turns out that smaller dogs live the longest. Corgis are small, and so they benefit from this weird factoid. One reason this might be is the fact that big dogs grow much faster than little ones. That means there is more opportunity for larger dogs to develop illnesses or diseases that shorten their lives. One of the biggest ways this shows itself is in viewing the cancer statistics of various breeds. Smaller dogs, on average, are far less likely to develop cancer.

Another important key for a longer living corgi is to consider where you purchase them. Pet stores or local dogs are often prone to issues with inbreeding, which lowers overall life expectancy by increasing the chances of medical problems. Purchasing a corgi from a respected breeder will eliminate this particular issue. Some people claim that a spayed dog lives longer; others claim that they don't live as long as unspayed dogs do. The numbers on this particular issue aren't clear; they give the impression that spaying or neutering has nothing to do with lifespan at all.

A corgi can be a friend of yours for many years, though they will still require your assistance to get over common ailments and to tackle hereditary diseases. We turn our attention to these now.

Common Ailments

While there are many ailments that a corgi may be afflicted with, the majority of them are going to come from hereditary diseases. The ailments which we'll look at in this section are those which are common to corgis (or dogs in general) but that don't arise from hereditary roots.

Allergies: Pretty much any dog can develop allergies. The result of an allergy can be a lot of doggy sneezes, but it can just as likely result in irritated skin, which the dog keeps biting or licking. Other possible fallouts from allergies are running noses, loss of weight or appetite, or other weird behaviors that seem outside of the norm for your corgi. Allergies are among the most common issues faced by corgis, but they are often easy to treat so long as you can find the cause.

If you suspect your corgi has allergies, then you can bring them into a vet to get them tested. That can cost a lot of money and take up a lot of time, so you may want to check your theory at home first to try to isolate the cause of the possible allergy. Remove items from the dog's environment one at a time to see if the ailment improves. It is important to only remove one at a time because if you remove more than one, it will take further testing to determine which item was the real culprit.

Allergies may also be caused by diet and food. If you have recently changed your dog's food, this would be the direction to start your investigation. Some pets take a little while to get used to a new food, and this shouldn't cause any worries, but if your corgi starts to demonstrate signs of allergies after switching, then the problem may not be the new taste, but the new ailment it triggers. Try switching the food to see if it helps. You'll want to keep an eye on the ingredients in the food you give your dogs; that way, you can begin to deduce what the cause was. Start by switching protein groups (from chicken to beef, for example) and then get into the smaller ingredients afterward. Keep in mind that testing food for allergies shouldn't occur at the same time you are experimenting with removing items from the environment, or it'll confuse the results.

Ear Infection: Dogs are particularly prone to issues with their ears due to the way that they are shaped. The inside of the ear canal has an odd shape, which allows infections to take hold easier, but the outside of the dog's ear may also account for part of the problem. When a dog is running around, and their ears are flopping, it is very easy for dust, dirt, and germs to get inside. These same infectants get removed naturally through airflow, but a dog with floppy ears that hang down when they rest cuts off this airflow.

While a corgi doesn't have any fewer problems with their ears compared to similar dogs, they are helped out by the fact that their ears aren't nearly as floppy. Instead, a corgi's ears like to point outwards, and this allows plenty of airflow to help clean them out. But this doesn't mean that they are immune to such issues. These treatable infections can be tackled so long as you know how to spot them. Thankfully, the signs of an ear infection are pretty clear.

If you notice that your corgi has begun to shake their head frequently or if you've noticed they're now scratching at their ears, this is a sign to take a closer look. You may notice some crusting in the ear or even some redness. Sometimes you might get lucky and notice some discharge from a distance. Any of these are signs to get your dog's ears treated. But, often, the most telling sign of all is silent. It requires you to get your nose close to the dog's ear and give it a sniff. A dog's ear doesn't smell good at the best of times, but when it is infected, it smells absolutely disgusting. Your nose will wrinkle, your gag reflex will kick in, and you will know without a doubt in the world that you need to get some treatment for your corgi. A vet will likely recommend treatment with ear drops.

Intervertebral Disc Disease: This particular issue happens because the discs between the vertebrae of the dog's spine begin to herniate and start to mess with the dog's spinal cord. This ailment can greatly reduce the mobility and agility of your corgi as if it suddenly aged many years. Corgis are at a higher risk of this particular ailment thanks to their long backs. This is particularly bad for corgis because, not only does it cause them pain, but it can even lead to paralysis if it is left untreated.

If your corgi is suffering from this, then you'll notice they suddenly seem a little drunk. You'll notice them weaving and wobbling, and they'll stop wanting to go up steps or to get up on the couch. In fact, you'll see that your corgi suddenly shows no interest in jumping at all. If you notice signs that your corgi's motor skills are being impaired, then you should take them into the vet and get it checked out immediately.

Obesity: We'll be covering diet and exercise later in the chapter, so if you follow the advice in those sections, then obesity shouldn't be a problem. But obesity is one of the standard health issues that any dog can face. The reason for this is simple: overweight dogs are cute, and feeding a dog feels like the right thing to do. But overweight dogs have a lot of health issues that fit dogs don't face.

Corgis are especially hit hard by obesity because of their small size. A golden retriever might be large enough to pack on a few extra pounds without seriously affecting their overall mood and energy levels, but a few extra pounds is a lot to a corgi. These dogs are only in the twenty-pound range, and so even two pounds sees a percentage of weight gained that's in the double digits. This extra weight causes issues for the legs, the joints, the heart, and other organs.

If you notice your corgi is putting on weight, then you should up the exercise and decrease the diet. If you see the weight gain is continuing regardless, then you should take your corgi to the vet for a checkup as the chances are good that there is something else causing the issue.

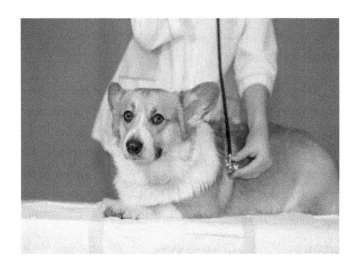

Hereditary Diseases Corgis Face

Hereditary diseases have a tendency to be much worse and scarier than those ailments we've explored above. These diseases find their roots in the corgi's history, puppies having inherited them from their mothers. It is these diseases that are most likely to cause the biggest headaches and heartaches when it comes to your dog.

Hip Dysplasia: This inherited problem affects far more than just corgis. Dogs like the golden retriever are also highly prone to this. As the dog grows, problems can arise with the joint of the hip. Each joint is made up of a ball that slots into a groove so that the joint can move and swivel around. Hip dysplasia is what we call it when either the ball or the slot are improperly sized. A ball too big for a slot will wear away at the bone and cause lasting damage.

Unfortunately, we aren't sure yet why hip dysplasia is an inherited condition. We also don't really know what environmental factors can make it worse. Our number one way of avoiding it is to not breed dogs with it. If you are purchasing your corgi from a respected breeder, then you can be sure that they came from stock that wasn't afflicted with this issue. But that doesn't mean that your corgi can't develop it naturally. Corgis have a tendency to develop arthritis as they get older. While arthritis isn't going to kill your dog, it can make issues like hip dysplasia more likely to occur.

If you notice that your dog is slower and having trouble with its hips, then you will want to take them to the vet and have them tested for hip dysplasia. Proper treatment and exercise can help to reduce the pain and restore function to the hip, though it is more a case of treating the symptoms rather than the cause. We just don't know enough yet to get down to the root of this particular genetic issue.

Eye Problems: Most dogs have issues with their eyes. What these particular issues are will change by breed, but eye problems unite many dogs. Corgis, in particular, are prone to getting progressive retinal atrophy, retinal dysplasia, or even plain old annoying cataracts. Treatment for these will all differ, but looking your corgi in the eye will let you catch them early.

Cataracts are the most typical of the eye issues. A cloudy milk-like substance covers the eye and makes it harder for light to get in. Since everything that we've ever seen is dependent on the way that light hits our eyes, it is easy to see how cataracts reduce vision and can even lead to blindness. Cataracts are one of those issues that show up more when a corgi is older. While not unheard of, it is rare for a young dog to develop them. Spot them early to be able to treat them or seek surgical care.

Corgis also have to deal with progressive retinal atrophy, which is a catch-all term used to describe a bunch of different eye issues. Basically, these diseases work together to destroy the retina of the dog's eye. Like cataracts, this can result in a blind corgi if you aren't careful. Unfortunately, this one is harder to spot than cataracts. The best sign that a corgi is suffering from progressive retinal atrophy will be the way they see at night. If you notice that your corgi begins to get clumsy at night, then it may be a sign that their retinas aren't working as they should. A dog with progressive retinal atrophy has less options for care compared to one with cataracts.

Retinal dysplasia is similar to hip dysplasia in that something is out of place. With the previously mentioned issue, that problem was the hip joint. With retinal dysplasia, the issue is that the retina can completely detach. This is a rare disease, but one that almost always results in blindness. If you catch it early, then this process can be slowed down, but it cannot be reversed. Spotting this one is hard since it can easily be confused with other issues that cause clumsiness, anxiety, or lack of energy. If you notice that your dog seems clumsier than normal, then it's a smart idea to get a vet's opinion sooner than later.

Von Willebrand Disease: This disease is common in many species of dog. It is also quite frequent in humans. It means that the blood in the corgi doesn't clot properly. Discovering this particular disease can be a scary experience because many owners don't realize their dog has it until they get cut and won't stop bleeding. This is a terrifying experience and one I hope you never encounter. The more common way that this disease is found is through surgery. A corgi goes in for an operation, and the doctors realize the animal has Von Willebrand disease based on the way their blood is slow to clot.

You could have a dog its entire life and not realize that it has Von Willebrand disease. This has happened to many dog owners. But Von Willebrand disease is scary because your corgi could just start bleeding from the nose or mouth. Sometimes there will even be blood in their feces. There are treatments that can make your dog much more comfortable and increase its longevity, but, unfortunately, it can't actually be cured.

The scariest part of this disease is the fact that your dog could just start bleeding and bleeding suddenly. It's rare, but some dogs with Von Willebrand disease will bleed to death without any triggering wound. If your corgi is bleeding for no discernible reason, take them to the vet and ask them to check for Von Willebrand disease. A simple DNA test will bring back a yes or no answer, and treatment can be planned from there.

Epilepsy: This is a tricky disease because it could fit into hereditary diseases or common ailments. The problem with epilepsy is that it is an inherited disease that may also occur naturally. That is, a dog with no history of epilepsy in its genes could still develop it.

Epilepsy is an issue of the brain which causes your corgi to have seizures. If you have never seen a dog have a seizure, then you probably aren't prepared for how scary it can be. Often it seems like your corgi is dying, and it isn't until they settle down that your nerves will begin to calm themselves. Seizures may manifest as frenzied running, twitches, a weaving walking pattern, or loss of consciousness. These can be very frightening, and if you witness any of them, then you should take your dog to the vet and tell them that you think it had a seizure. They'll test it for epilepsy and let you know about treatment. If it isn't epilepsy, then the chances are there is an allergen causing the fits.

If your corgi has epilepsy, the good news is that there is a lot that medical science can do to treat it and keep it in check. Epilepsy left untreated can lead to worse health issues down the road or even death.

Exercising a Corgi: Body and Mind

Corgis are big dogs in small bodies. We often think of work dogs as being big breeds, but the corgi was first bred as a herding dog, and so they're used to hard work. This gives them a sense of pride like a big dog. But it also means that a corgi needs to be exercised like a big dog, too. In order to give a corgi enough exercise, we'll look at how much they need to keep them strong. Remember, too, that corgis are intelligent dogs as well. Because of this, we'll also be providing exercise for their brain. While it isn't a muscle, a corgi's brain needs to be worked out just like their bodies do.

A corgi should be walked at least daily. Often, walking twice a day is a better idea. The reason that twice a day is suggested is because most people don't consider the length of the walk itself. To many people, walking the dog means taking them for a ten or fifteen-minute stroll around the neighborhood. This is better than getting no exercise at all, but it isn't enough for a healthy, young corgi. Your corgi is going to want at least an hour of exercise every day. If walking is your main way of exercising your corgi, then you should be out there for at least 45 minutes a day.

Daily walks are the most common way of getting your corgi the exercise it needs, but this alone isn't enough. Corgis need some time running and playing and burning up all of that extra energy. Puppies will have more energy than older dogs, and older dogs will start to need less and less exercise every year as they become less inclined to rush about, and their bodies get more tender and sore. It is important to exercise your corgi as recommended for their age, as too much exercise can cause issues in the joints and muscles. Over-exercising can also lead to issues like heatstroke. If you are exercising outside, then bring a bowl and some water with you if possible. If you can't bring a bowl, a carefully poured water bottle can achieve the same effect.

Along with the walks, activities like fetch can be great ways to burn energy and get exercise. Taking your corgi to an off-leash dog park will make them very happy, as they'll be able to run and play independently. You may think about getting a set of herding balls for the dog. These balls are designed for play with herding dogs so that they can work out those natural instincts. You can make this an even better exercise by adding some weight to the balls so that your corgi needs to flex its muscles a little harder. Along with herding balls are plain old tennis balls. Corgis love to play fetch as much as any dog, and this can burn lots of energy. Toys that move on their own are great since they play chase with the dog without you having to do anything. Other activities that make for great workouts include playing tug of war, swimming, or jumping. These simple activities can burn a lot of energy and give your corgi a fantastic workout.

All of these are good for the body, but we can't forget the brain. We mentioned hidden treat games in chapter three when discussing leaving a corgi at home alone. Toys like these require the corgi to follow its nose and use its wits to solve minor puzzles. These might seem like simple toys, but they teach the dog how to maneuver small objects and follow their senses. This makes for smarter dogs. But if you're already training your dog, then you are offering the best mental exercise possible. Regardless of age, you should try to train your corgi throughout its entire life. Learning new tricks and commands will force the corgi's gears to turn. The result of that is a smart corgi. Plus, who doesn't love showing off new tricks?

A Diet for a Corgi

Corgis are small dogs, and so, on average, they tend to be between 22 and 27 pounds. Despite this small size, they use up lots of energy, and so they require a diet more in tune with a bigger dog. That said, it should be remembered that every dog is different. I could offer you guidelines for feeding your corgi, only for you to discover that they are allergic to one of the recommendations. Or you may have a corgi that has medical issues and isn't able to exercise much. A corgi like this wouldn't need to eat as much as a more active one. These minor differences will change things, but, generally, a corgi of standard weight that gets enough exercise will need close to 800 calories a day. Puppies will need to eat more than adult dogs, but this doesn't mean more food in their bowl. What it means is that they'll need more calories per pound. If your puppy is 15 pounds, then it might eat as much as a 25-pound corgi does. This wouldn't be more food in itself, but it is a higher ratio of food-per-pound.

So, if a corgi needs close to 800 calories a day, we know how *much* they need to eat. But we still don't know *what* they need to eat. For that, we can look at the diets of dogs in general. As it turns out, a corgi doesn't have a unique diet as a breed, but they might have different diets when considered on a corgi by corgi basis. With that said, we should be ensuring that the food we select is high in protein and fat.

We select a high protein because this is used to help the corgi's muscles to grow and function properly. The best foods will use two or more meats in order to get their proteins. When you look at the package, you want these meats to be among the first ingredients listed. That tells you there are lots of them present. Chicken, fish, lamb, and beef are all fine choices. For fat, you'll want to find sources that are clearly listed. Some packaging will just put the fat content, but this shouldn't be enough for you or your little corgi. Select food that tells you where the fat came from. Also, go for foods that include essential fats like omega-3 fatty acids. Omega-3 will help with the corgi's coat, while the named fat is a necessary part of its diet.

While you are looking at the ingredients, steer clear of foods that list corn, wheat, or soy. These fillers don't sit well with a corgi. Other forms of grain, such as rice or oats, are fine to include. You should also look to see if the packaging lists ash. More common in cat food, ash is a cheap filler that dry foods often use to keep costs down. Unfortunately, this has the side effect of increasing dietary and health issues.

The best way to feed a dog is to use a combination of dry food and wet food. The wet food has a stronger scent and taste, so put it at the bottom of the bowl. That way, your corgi needs to eat through the dry food to get at the wet. The wet food will also help the dry food to digest easier.

If you follow these steps in choosing the right dog food for your corgi, then you'll be providing them with the proper nutrition. If you combine these lessons with those we've covered on exercise, then you'll have yourself one healthy corgi. Remember to keep an eye out for common ailments and hereditary diseases. If you do so, then you'll be able to catch them early and provide your vet with all the necessary information to protect your canine pal.

Chapter Summary

- The oldest corgi on record lived to be 29.

- The average lifespan of a corgi is between 12 to 15 years.

- Larger animals live much longer than small ones, but when it comes to dogs, this is reversed. Little dogs like corgis can live much longer lives than larger breeds like golden retrievers.

- Purchasing a corgi from a respected breeder results in a dog with a much better life expectancy than one from a pet store. This is because a respected breeder would never resort to inbreeding.

- Corgis are prone to allergies, the same as most dogs. If you start to notice itching, sneezing, excessive biting, or licking, then your corgi may have allergies.

- A vet can run tests to see if your corgi is allergic to anything, but you can also run your own at home. Remove one item at a time from the dog's environment and see if the situation improves.

- Food allergies may also develop over time. If this happens, then you are going to want to switch foods to something with a different protein source. Just remember not to test food at the same time you are looking for environmental triggers.

- Ear infections are common in all canines due to the way their ear canals are shaped.

- If you notice your corgi is shaking its head or scratching at an ear a lot, then this is a sign of an ear infection. Upon examination, you might find redness or other signs of infection, but the clearest sign is a disgusting smell coming from the ear.

- Ear infections will cause your dog a lot of discomfort, but they are easily treatable.

- Intervertebral disc disease is an issue in which the discs of the dog's spine begin to herniate. Your dog might even look like it's drunk. This can produce a lot of pain and discomfort, and you should take your corgi to the vet if you suspect it.

- Fat dogs may seem cute, but obesity is nothing to laugh about. A corgi doesn't have a body designed to carry extra weight, and so a few extra pounds can equal a ton of health problems down the road.

- Hip dysplasia is a hereditary disease in which either the ball or the socket of the hip joint becomes mismatched, and they no longer slot together as they should. This seriously affects your corgi's mobility.

- Eye problems are common in dogs. Corgis have to deal with cataracts, retinal dysplasia, and progressive retinal atrophy. Each of these horrible ailments can cause blindness if they aren't treated. Make sure to check your corgi's eyes regularly, and be aware of how much confidence they show moving around in the dark or going up and down stairs.

- Von Willebrand disease is a hereditary issue that causes your dog's blood to fail to clot properly. A simple cut could require a blood transfusion when your doggy's got this common ailment.

- Epilepsy can be a hereditary disease, but it can also just develop by itself. It results in your corgi having seizures, and these can be quite scary. Thankfully, epilepsy in dogs rarely leads to death, and it can be managed easily with modern medicine.

- A corgi needs to be walked at least once a day. This walk should be for a minimum of 45 minutes. If you can't take your dog for this long in one go, then take them out for two walks daily.

- Playing fetch or spending time with herding balls will be great for your corgi. They also love getting a chance to play at the dog park without a leash on, since it helps to placate their independent nature.

- You should also train your corgi's mind by continuing to teach them commands and tricks and by getting them puzzle toys that challenge them.

- A corgi may be a small dog, but they still need to eat around 800 calories a day.

- Corgis who aren't very active will need to eat slightly less each day.

- We should be picking foods that are high in protein, and with sources clearly listed near the top of the ingredient list.

- Omega-3 fatty acids are also a great addition to a corgi's diet since it helps keep their fur looking healthy.

- Avoid foods that have corn, wheat, soy, or ash listed in the ingredients.

- A combination of dry and wet food makes for the best diet. The wet food will make them want to keep eating, while also making the dry food easier on the digestive tract.

In the next chapter, you will learn how to train your corgi. We'll begin by looking at just how trainable these little guys are; after all, they really are stubborn and can present some roadblocks when being taught. Thankfully, you'll learn that these are easy to get around with a little time and patience. We'll learn how we teach our corgis basic commands and how we can use a clicker in their training if we like.

CHAPTER SIX

HOW TO TRAIN YOUR CORGI

Training a corgi isn't an easy experience. If you've never trained a dog before, then starting with a corgi isn't a brilliant idea. These little fellows are independent and stubborn. They've got lots of energy, too, so it can be hard to get them to stop and pay attention. If you can get your training to stick with a corgi, then you are going to have a much easier time training them throughout the rest of their lives. But if you can't get training to stick when they're young, then you may never be able to succeed at it. These dogs often end up outsmarting their owners. Often the corgi turns out to be the one doing the teaching.

In this chapter, we'll spend some time considering the trainability of corgis. What makes them easier to train? What makes them harder? These give us a clear picture of the ways we can make our lives easier when it comes to our corgi's training routine. We'll move from here onto the basic commands that your corgi (and, really, every dog) should know. Sit, come, halt, and no are all core commands that will make your life with a dog a thousand times easier. Finally, we'll close out on a discussion of clicker training.

Trainability

If you want to bring a dog into your life, then you are going to want them to be trained. You may be the one responsible for this training or you may hire another to do it, the means isn't as important as the end result. We don't want a dog that refuses to listen; this is just an invitation for frustration. Corgis are vastly intelligent dogs, and this means they can easily learn new commands and training. Though the "easily" part might be a bit of a lie. They have the *ability* to easily learn, but more often than not, a corgi makes this a hard experience due to the way they're so strongly independent.

If you want to train a corgi, then you are going to need to start when they're a puppy. If you wait too long, then the corgi is going to form its own behaviors, schedules, and routines. Once these are in place, they can be nearly impossible to break. The earlier you can get started, the more likely you are to find success. If you are adopting a fully grown corgi, look for one that has already been trained, as this will make your life easier. If you are looking to adopt a puppy, then it is better to go younger, as you'll have more time to work on getting the training to stick. You should also start pretty much as soon as the puppy is yours and in your home. Give them a day, two at most, so they can explore the house and meet everyone. Once the puppy feels safe enough to explore on its own and hang out with the family, then you can start training.

Training should be done on a daily basis. Try not to ever skip a day, especially not after the corgi has done a good job learning. You may think it makes sense to reward your corgi with a day off, but this is going to make it harder for you to teach your dog. Instead, set time aside each day to train. You'll want to plan these ahead of time, as training at the same time every day will make it easier for the puppy to see training as part of its daily routine. We do the same thing by scheduling when we feed our puppies, and when we take them out to pee. Creating routine is extremely important for a corgi puppy. If you don't create it, they will, and then you'll be forever beholden to their whims.

You want to make sure that the dog understands the schedule. Once they do, you can start adding obedience training into their routine. This includes all those commands that we'll be covering next. It is also the hardest part of training a corgi because of that independent streak. When you first start teaching them, you may notice that they don't seem to be following or obeying. In fact, even after a corgi has learned a command, you may find they pretend they don't remember. Adolescent corgis will do this, as dogs of this age like to test the bounds of their relationship to their human. Basically, an adolescent dog is a teenager, and that brings with it lots of issues. But, regardless of whether your corgi is a puppy or an adolescent, you should continue to train every day even when they aren't doing that well. Furthermore, you should also never stop a training session early because of the dog's behavior or attitude. When you do this, you show the dog that it controls you and not the other way around. Try to be patient and offer positive reinforcement to strengthen the neurology around the command.

If you keep up this training, then you will be able to train your corgi. However, keep in mind that at no point have we discussed a timeline for training. Everyone has questions like, "How long will I need to train my corgi before he gets it?" But nobody can answer this accurately. This is determined on a dog by dog basis. Consider training from a human standpoint. How long it would take you to learn to paint is going to be determined by a whole lot of different factors. The simplest painting in the world might be extremely difficult for you, but not for another person. Training a dog is like this. You just don't know what your dog is going to be good at, bad at, or indifferent to until you start their training. Have patience, take your time, and don't give up. Corgis are absolutely trainable, but if you throw in the towel first, then you'll never get there.

Basic Commands

Depending on what your rules are, you are going to want to use different commands than those listed here. However, most of those we'll be looking into are must-haves for any dog. But what basic commands you want are as unique as you and your dog's relationship. I might allow my dog up on the couch while you wouldn't. This means that I would have no need to teach them the "get down" command, but you would. As you consider training your corgi, look at the commands explored below and choose those that are relevant to your needs. At the minimum, you should teach sit, come, stay, and no. On the other hand, remember, too, that training is good for your corgi's mind. You may want to keep teaching them as many commands as possible, simply to keep up your training sessions and the dog's mental stimulation.

Sit: Sit is one of the most essential commands, and it is pretty easy to teach. Most training begins with sit because it can be used as a foundation for more commands. For example, if you wanted to teach your corgi to shake hands, then you would first have them sit so that they could raise a paw. Lie down is similar, in that it is easier to teach once they know the sit command. To teach this command, hold a treat out to your dog so that they can smell it. Once they want the snack, push down on their hindquarters while saying, "sit." Do this until the dog sits, at which point you can give them their treat. It may take you several sessions of pushing the dog's butt down, but they will grasp the meaning of the command with a little bit of patience and positive reinforcement.

Come: This can be a harder one to teach, but it is equally as important as sit, despite the fact that this command isn't part of any foundational commands the same way the sit command is. Instead, "come" is closer to the "stay" command in that it helps to eliminate possible issues. If your corgi gets out of your home, gets off the leash, or just starts pestering the neighbors, then the come command is used to get them to return to you. This is super-important because nobody wants a corgi to get out and then be hit by a car. You want to be able to give this command and have the corgi turn tail and return to you immediately. The best way to impose this instruction is by initially teaching the dog to stay. Tie a rope around the dog's collar. Hold the rope at a distance and tell them to come. If they don't, then give it a gentle tug to get them to come towards you while saying come. Reward them when they get to you and then start again. This is one of the longest and hardest of the basic commands when it comes to corgis because they are so free-spirited, but if you can get them to follow this one, then you can teach them virtually anything.

Down: If you want to keep your corgi off the furniture, then this is the command for you. It is also a good one to teach if you have a dog that likes to jump all over people, though corgis don't tend to do this as much since they're so small they wouldn't reach above your waist. It can be quite difficult to teach your corgi this particular command because of that independent steak. Sometimes worded as "lay down" or "go lay down," what you are essentially telling the dog is to put itself in a submissive position. In doing so, you are fundamentally telling the dog you are more powerful than it is. A corgi can have a hard time accepting this. The best way to teach this is to take a treat and let the dog smell it. Once the corgi knows the treat is there, put your hand down to the floor while giving the command. Your corgi is probably going to want to stick its nose after your hand, but we want them to lay down, so use your other hand to gently push on its body while repeating the command. Once the corgi lies down, give them the treat and some pets. You will need to practice this command daily. It will be much easier to teach this command if you've already got this next one in place.

No!: This is a powerful command, one that should leave no doubt in your dog's mind as to what you are feeling. To that end, the exclamation mark is certainly deserved. If your corgi is doing something they're not supposed to, then it's this command that you'll use to get them to knock it off. However, this is a bit of a weird one to teach. This command doesn't come with treats or particular uses such as down. Instead, this command is taught instinctually. Your corgi is intelligent, and so they'll be able to read your emotions and your energy. When you give a "No!" command, you need to make sure that it comes from deep within your stomach so that it has a deep bass rumble. Say it forcefully and loud, with an authority that lets the corgi know you are not in any mood to play. If done correctly, your corgi will cut out whatever they are doing. This particular command needs to be practiced, but it only works when the dog is doing something it isn't supposed to. You can't train "No!" without something for the dog to stop doing; otherwise, it will only confuse them.

Stay: Finally, we come to stay. Stay is a fantastic command that acts a lot like the come command does. But rather than get a corgi that has run away to come, the stay command is used to prevent them from running away in the first place. This is one of those commands which requires your corgi to do more than just listen to what you say. When you tell a corgi to stay, what you are saying is, "Stay where you are despite the fact that you want to run off." So you are telling your dog not to listen to its primal instincts. This makes it a particularly tricky command for a dog to learn because it needs to rewire its brain to pull it off. But with practice and patience, a corgi can learn and master this particular skill. Start by telling the corgi to sit down. Then, show your dog a treat while saying stay. If he starts to come towards you, then use the "No!" command and tell them to sit again and stay. Show them the treat while saying stay. If your corgi listens this time, then take a step backward and show them the treat again. Repeat the command. If they stay this time, then give them the treat. The goal with this command is to increase the distance between you and the dog, so that they understand this is a command they need to follow even when you aren't standing right next to them. Also, make sure that you change the length of time the corgi is told to stay. If you use the same length of time whenever you practice, then those parameters will be learned, and your corgi will think that stay means "Stay where you are for ten seconds" and not "Stay until I tell you to come." By changing the length of time and the distance from you that the dog stays, you make sure they learn that the command is the crucial part and not the rest of the factors in play.

111

Contemplating Clicker Training

Clicker training has been taking off lately as an alternative way of training your dogs. In my opinion, clicker training isn't any better or worse than the traditional training we have been discussing in the previous section. In our teachings, we talked about interacting with the dog and using our words, voice, and body to convey meanings such as sit (we say it while pushing the dog's butt down) or "No!" (which is closer to a phatic expression than a real word). These commands require us to interact with the dog and to give them the signal for what they need to do. Clicker training completely changes this.

With clicker training, you have a small clicker, which makes a simple sound each time you press it. As you teach your corgi new commands, you time the use of the clicker so that when the dog properly demonstrates the command, you make a clicking noise. This teaches the dog to connect the clicking noise to the treat and the action. This works to create an association through positive reinforcement. Once the dog knows this, they will follow through with the command when they hear the clicker. So, instead of having to say sit, you can teach them sit with a clicker, and then use the clicker to get them to sit later on. To us, this clicking noise has no meaning, but to the dog, it has the same meaning as "sit." Basically, we're just talking gibberish to our dogs anyway, and so they don't really know the difference between a spoken command and a clicked one. The more you use a clicker, the more effective it is, and there's plenty of evidence that shows it to be at least as effective as traditional training.

Some owners claim that clicker training is easier and more effective than traditional. These owners will talk for ages about why it is so much better. But what they are really explaining is why it is better for them, rather than for training as a whole. As mentioned, the clicker is used at the same time as your dog correctly following a command. This teaches them to associate with the clicker; then, you can press on the clicker to get the command later. This cuts out a second or two of having to speak to the dog. That might be a minor time-saver, but it isn't particularly noteworthy in a book specifically about corgis. Other benefits that are often mentioned are the fact that you can teach this method to kids as a straightforward way to get them interacting with the dog. The fact that you can start to phase clickers out overtime is also mentioned, as well as the idea that clicker training is a good way to improve your dog training skills. But again, nothing about corgis.

The most interesting benefit that owners of corgis are going to get out of clicker training is the fact that you can start it earlier than most training. When you first begin to teach a puppy, they need to learn to understand your voice so that they can tell when you're angry and when you're happy. Then a puppy needs to sort out all of the different sounds they hear to pinpoint that "sit" or "come" or whatever command you are using is the one they need to follow. Finally, they use their eyes to try to read and understand you, but they're puppies, and so they don't understand humans yet, let alone a particular one. But a clicker is just a single sound, a click, and this makes it very simple to understand. You still need to use spoken commands and suggestions (like pushing their tushie) when training a puppy with a clicker, but the click helps to sink the lessons in. Since we want to train corgis while they're young and malleable, clicker training may offer one way of making the process easier and less frustrating so that you can get straight to what matters, instead of getting caught up in a tangle of words, phrases, and misunderstood intentions.

Chapter Summary

- Training a corgi isn't easy, but it is entirely possible.

- These dogs are intelligent and stubborn, and they often beat their owners when it comes to a battle of wits (or training!).

- This intelligence makes corgis able to learn lots of great commands, as well as make them ideal partners for tackling work.

- But this intelligence and stubbornness also mean you need to be constantly demonstrating lots of patience and understanding while training.

- Start a corgi's training when they're young, or they'll form routines and behaviors which are hard, if not impossible, to break.

- You should train a corgi daily. By doing that, they'll get used to the schedule so that they look forward to trying. It also creates an expectation for the dog and helps them understand their role in what is happening.

- Training your corgi is going to require time and effort. It may take a couple of weeks to get the basics down. But as long as you keep coming back and training the dog, it will happen.

- Adolescent corgis can be frustrating because they act like they don't know their commands anymore. Continue training your corgi every single day, and don't give up on a session because the dog isn't into it. When you give up, you end up being controlled by your dog.

- You are going to want to train basic commands like sit and stay.

- Start with training sit, as this is then used for other commands like stay.

- Teaching a corgi to lie down is incredibly difficult because it goes against everything the dog's nature is telling it to do. Keep at it again and again. It will eventually sink in. Once you see that you can teach even the hardest of tricks, the rest is a piece of cake.

- "No!" is a powerful command which doesn't need to be trained so much as it needs to be felt. Always speak with authority when using this command.

- Clicker training uses a simple noise, a click, to help reinforce your corgi's training. While clicker training isn't necessarily any better or worse than traditional training, it can allow you to start teaching the dog earlier, and this can be a blessing when it comes to corgis.

In the next chapter, you will learn how to discipline your corgi. While the word discipline sounds like it involves punishment, what it requires is reinforcement: the training of their mind through treats, praise, and repetition. More than any way to discipline a dog, this is the one that nets the best results.

CHAPTER SEVEN

DISCIPLINING YOUR CORGI

When we hear the word discipline, we often think of punishment. However, disciplining doesn't necessarily involve punishment. Or, when it does, it doesn't require that punishment be in the form of threats or abuse. I'm sure I'm right in thinking that you wouldn't dream of abusing your corgi, but there are too many people out there that have done exactly this. Corgis are challenging to train because of their stubbornness, and this can make many owners frustrated. They often claim that their corgi is too dumb to understand commands and that abuse or force is the only thing they do understand.

This is simply wrong.

What is happening, in this case, is a person is blaming their dog for their own weaknesses and failures. The corgi didn't fail to learn. You failed to train it. This is a fault of you and not the dog, and so the dog doesn't deserve to be hurt or made to feel bad for its inability. At the end of the day, it is simply a dog. It is trying to be your friend and get exercise and food and enjoy its life. It wants to be close to you, and it doesn't have the ability to understand that it has done you wrong in any way. This would be the last thing in the world that your poor little fluff-ball would ever want.

When you teach a dog that you'll hurt it if it does something, you are using a form of reinforcement. However, you aren't reinforcing the behavior that you are trying to change. What you are reinforcing in the dog's mind is the fact that you are scary and will hurt it. It might not get on the couch anymore with this kind of reinforcement, but the motive will be based on fear. It has nothing to do with learning that the couch is off-limits and everything to do with the fact the dog doesn't want you to hurt it. Meanwhile, a well-trained dog learns to understand the down command and then take pride in themselves when they listen. They learn the command and the behavior, and they are left feeling good about it.

Our goal is to create this second response and to do so, we primarily use positive reinforcement. We add a tiny splash of negative reinforcement to make the positive reinforcement stronger, but this negative reinforcement should never threaten or physically harm the corgi.

Understanding Reinforcement

Reinforcement is a very, very powerful tool. So powerful, in fact, that you can use it to train yourself, let alone a corgi. When we do something right, and we get rewarded, as humans, we can understand what we did and why it worked and all the various and complex interpersonal relationships that allowed the thing to go right in the first place. A dog doesn't understand this. A dog simply realizes that it gets a treat when it does what you tell it to. But the cool part about this is that your corgi is actually demonstrating the same learning technique that your mind does. If you are trying to learn a new habit, reward yourself with a sugary snack afterward. This will teach your subconscious and your body itself that it gets a gift for doing the right behavior. You've used positive reinforcement on yourself since a treat (the positive) is being used to reinforce the behavior that you want to continue.

If it is powerful enough that we can use it to train ourselves, then it is most definitely powerful enough to teach our corgis. The best part is that dogs are already so food-focused. When we use a treat to train ourselves, we have to remember to go get it. If you're hungry, then this is easy to do, but if you're busy, you can easily forget. Dog's don't forget about food. Ever. If you show your corgi a treat, then they are going to be determined to get that snack, no matter what. That's great because your dog is going to want to learn and reinforce the behavior.

Let's take a look at what is happening inside the dog's brain. It isn't consciously thinking, "I need to sit my backside down in order to get a treat." Instead, positive reinforcement begins with a bunch of variables in play. Your tone, the words you say, what is happening in the environment, what noises are going on around, and how your dog acts are just some of the factors which the dog's brain needs to sort through to figure out what is happening. When it sits on command for the first time and gets a treat, it isn't going to be able to tell that sitting was the action that resulted in the treat. There were too many things happening for any one in particular to be picked out. But as you continue to reinforce this training, the variables present at each training session are going to be different, but the ones that are the same are your command, the action the dog takes, and the fact that it receives a reward. As you practice training, these connections are strengthened because they always result in a reward. Thus, the subconscious and biology of the dog work together so as to get the new teaching to stick.

If we try to teach this same behavior with threats and abuse, then what the dog learns is that sitting down results in a beating. Of course, people that hurt their animals are more likely to beat a dog because it didn't listen rather than because it did. So if this is the case, then you tell the dog to sit, it doesn't sit, and so it gets beaten. What has the dog learned? It hasn't learned to sit. It hasn't even learned what sit means. Instead, it learns to associate the word with the beating. Other environmental factors that are present can also easily get confused in this manner since there is no positive reinforcement of the successful behavior. Instead, there is a beating. This teaches the dog to be afraid and confused. Abusing a dog never results in a well-trained dog, only a broken and scared one.

With that said, it is worth realizing that there is such a thing as negative reinforcement, and it can be used exceedingly well to help with training and teaching. Pretend that you've come home to find your corgi chewing on your favorite pair of shoes. That's going to make you angry, and your first desire might be to scare, hurt, or scold the dog. Scolding is okay, but unless you catch them in the act, they won't even know why they are being told off. A better solution is to use negative reinforcement to teach a lesson. If the dog chews on your shoe, then you take away its chew toy for a while. You take something away from the dog as a punishment. Doing that means you don't hurt the dog, but it does still help to discipline them. Just make sure that you take away something that the dog likes, but not something they need. You should never deny a dog a meal just because it did something you didn't like. This is cruel, and rather than helping to train the dog, it has a high chance of leaving them sick or undernourished.

Using reinforcement to train a dog is the best way to get the lessons to take properly, but it requires patience and understanding. Your dog might learn to stay off the couch quicker if you rely on force, but this doesn't actually train the dog. Instead, you should mentally promise your corgi that you are going to treat it properly and be mindful of the way you use reinforcement. Reinforcement is one of those things that happen whether we are aware of it or not. When we aren't aware of it, we often end up reinforcing the wrong things, but by being aware, we can make sure to only reinforce those behaviors which we approve of and desire.

Chapter Summary

- Discipline evokes ideas of punishment, but discipline is merely the process of teaching someone, or a corgi, to follow the rules.

- Corgis are independent and stubborn creatures. This can make training them frustrating. But no matter how frustrated you are, there is never a good reason to abuse or hurt your dog.

- The best way to train a corgi is to use positive reinforcement. This makes the neural pathways in the dog's head stronger by using rewards to reinforce the teachings you desire. This same technique can be used to train yourself, too.

- When we abuse our dogs, we teach them to be afraid. We don't teach them to listen to our commands; we teach them to fear what happens if they get in our way. That is a dreadful thing to inflict on a dog.

- Negative reinforcement can be a powerful tool, such as taking away a chew toy when your corgi has decided to chew on your shoes instead. But negative reinforcement should never take away food, water, or anything else your corgi needs to stay fit and healthy.

In the next chapter, you will learn all about the life cycle of the corgi. From puppy to adolescence, and adolescence to adult, we look at the three major cycles that your corgi goes through.

CHAPTER EIGHT

THE LIFE CYCLE OF A CORGI

In this chapter, we're going to take a quick look at the life cycle of a corgi. From cute puppy to adorable adult, there are three stages of life that each corgi passes through. This is the same for many dogs, even following roughly the same timeframe. Please note, however, that individual dogs may take longer or shorter amounts of time to progress. In particular, the grey area of adolescence is unpredictable. We'll look at each of these stages before moving on to some final words so you can get back to training your new corgi.

Corgi Puppies (0-1.5 years)

Corgi puppies are adorable and precious. They stay in the womb for about two months. When born, corgis are so tiny it is unbelievable. For the first two months of their lives, they can't leave the house since they require the assistance of their mother. The mother corgi teaches the dogs how to eat, speak, walk, and interact with the world. It is through watching their mother that corgis first learn about being friends with humans.

At about the time that you adopt a corgi, they should be somewhere between nine and thirteen pounds. Their weight increases steadily so that you can notice a week by week difference. At four months, you can expect them in the twelve to sixteen-pound range. This continues quickly until around eight months, at which point they still grow, but so slowly that you might not even notice a difference from month to month.

Puppies need to eat more food than an adult dog, and they need lots and lots of exercise. But, just as importantly, this is the stage that you want to begin their training. The earlier you start the training, the better the experience is going to be. One reason for this is that your corgi puppy is going to be an adolescent corgi soon, and trying to teach an adolescent corgi can be a nightmare, even after a foundation of training has been put in place.

Adolescent Corgis (6 months - two years)

Adolescence occurs somewhere between six months and two years. Technically this means that your corgi can still be a puppy while going through part of adolescence. These may seem to contradict each other, but we see this same thing happen in humans. Is a 12-year-old a kid or a teenager? In a way, they're sorta both. Corgis may enter adolescence in a middle state like this, but they finish growing and become adults by the time they're done.

Adolescence for a corgi is confusing to try to talk about in much depth. Mostly this is because you can't be sure when it is going to hit. It might hit at month six; it might not hit until month twelve. At some point, it is going to arrive, and you are going to know it. With a corgi, since they're a rather small dog, they are more likely to enter into this stage earlier rather than later as a larger dog might.

A teenage corgi is going to be a nightmare to train. If you have already started to train them as a puppy, then it will be a little easier, but not very much. Teenage corgis like to act like they forgot what they were taught. They want to misbehave and get into trouble. This happens to corgis for the same reason that it happens to humans: hormones.

A puppy doesn't have many hormones pumping through it when it's little, but once it is old enough, they start to come out in force. These hormones are doing to the dog the same thing they're doing to the human:

making them want to go out and mate. The smartest thing biology did was make it an animal instinct to procreate. Adolescent corgis want to be parents, despite the fact that they're not yet adults.

It is around this stage that many owners get their dogs neutered. A neutered dog doesn't have the same hormonal problems, but if you wait until they are acting out, you've moved too slow. If you are already planning on having your corgi neutered, then you should try to get it done before they start acting all hormonal, as this can help to reduce the awkwardness of this stage.

One sign that your corgi is entering into this stage of life will be their shedding. Puppies only have a single coat of fur, and so they don't need to shed very much. But once puppies start to hit adolescence, that puppy coat comes off. Suddenly there is hair everywhere because they need to shed it all off so they can make room for the coat they'll have the rest of their lives. That can be a good sign that it is time to get your puppy neutered. This is because neutered dogs usually shed for about two months after the operation as the hormones in their body settle. If your puppy is already shedding, then this can be a great way to double up so that you don't need to deal with as much shedding for as long of a period otherwise.

You'll find that your corgi begins to settle down as they start to approach a year and a half to two years of age. It is around this age that your corgi falls into the rhythms that will fuel the rest of its adult life.

Adult Corgis (2 years - 20 years)

Finally, we come to adult corgis. We've been looking at information about these little guys throughout the book, so there isn't a whole lot to say. Somewhere around the two-year mark, your corgi will seemingly straighten up and listen to you again as it mellows into adulthood, and the silliness of adolescence is left behind. Don't be surprised if this seems to happen as early as a year and a half old; smaller dogs have a tendency to move through these stages quickly, and so a smaller corgi won't take as long as a larger one does.

The amount of food and exercise that a corgi needs settles back down at this point. As a puppy and an adolescent, a corgi needs tons of exercise and food. While these are both still important (and covered in chapter five), they don't need nearly as much, and so it might feel like you are finally getting your time back since you first adopted a new corgi.

If you continue to feed and exercise your corgi correctly, you will be able to keep its body in a healthy condition. It is essential you don't forget about their minds. Corgis are smart dogs, and so they need mental stimulation to excel. Many people think that training their corgi stops once they have the basic commands or once they are an adult. This isn't and shouldn't be the case. If you continue to train your corgi, you will continue to exercise its mind.

A corgi stays an adult through the rest of its life. For the most part, this is unremarkable. But the older the corgi gets, the more likely it is going to have to deal with some medical issues. This is all part of aging, no matter what species you are. But as your corgi gets older, you'll have had plenty of years with them in which you've learned what they like, what they don't like, what behaviors are normal, and what behaviors are odd. You might be noticing more and more strange behaviors as the years tick on, but unless these point towards one of the medical issues we looked at, you are probably fine.

Remember to take your corgi to see the vet at least once a year for a checkup.

If you've followed the advice in this book, then you could easily have a decade and a half with your corgi pal, I hope that they're wonderful years.

Chapter Summary

- There are three major stages of life that a corgi moves through: puppy, adolescence, and adulthood.

- Corgi puppies stay with their mother for the first two months. This lets them learn how to be a dog before they are adopted.

- Start training a corgi puppy as soon as you can. If you own the mother corgi, then you can start even earlier than two months.

- Corgis should weigh between nine and thirteen points when you adopt them. They will continue to grow until they are around 25 pounds, their adult weight. That should happen around the eighth to the tenth month, though they aren't yet an adult.

- Puppies need more food and exercise than an adult dog does.

- Adolescent corgis are like moody teenagers. They are more likely to try to rail against their training, and they can get an attitude problem. This is due to the hormones blasting through their bodies.

- Adolescence can be made easier by spaying your corgi beforehand. This will prevent the moodiness that comes from the hormones.

- It is in adolescence that a corgi sheds its puppy coat, and starts to grow its double coat of fur. There will be a lot of shedding.

- Adult corgis settle down a lot compared to what they're like in adolescence.

- A corgi can hit adulthood in as little as a year and a half after being born.

- As a corgi gets older, it will face more and more health issues. This is a natural (though sad) part of life.

FINAL WORDS

Corgis are among the most intelligent breeds there are when it comes to dogs, but this is accompanied by a tendency to be fiercely stubborn. These dogs have been workers since they were first discovered, helping out on the farms by herding cattle and keeping them safe from predators. These were important jobs at the time, though now corgis have gone from workers to loving members of our families. Their cute, wiggly butts have been shared in thousands of GIFs across the web to bring amusement and joy to millions of people. They make a beautiful addition to a family, as I'm sure you'll find out yourself.

You need to remember the responsibility that a new puppy brings. You need to start teaching them early, or you'll never end up getting the lessons to stick. You also need to remember the fact that your young corgi doesn't understand what is happening, it is still a puppy, and so it needs to learn how the world works. That's where you play the most prominent role. You can choose to teach them from a place of patience and understanding, or you can choose to teach them through fear and abuse. I hope those last two ideas sicken you as much as they do me.

Corgis are notorious for shedding and are stubborn learners. Many people think these traits make them undesirable. But if you follow the advice in chapter four, then you can get around the shedding problem through thoughtful, daily brushing sessions. You also know from chapter six that corgis are absolutely trainable; you just need to start them young and have plenty of patience. The big thing with training a corgi is not to give up. When you give up, the corgi wins, and it trains you instead. Don't let them win; they're a tenth of your size after all.

It is my deepest hope that you bring a corgi puppy into your family so that you can see first-hand the happiness and joy they can bring. So long as you are sure that you can meet their needs such as not being left alone too long, being fed a healthy diet, and exercised for at least forty-five minutes a day, then I am sure that you will have a wonderful time with the newest, furriest member of your family. They are family, after all, don't forget that. They are a member of the family, and they deserve to be respected and treated as such. But I already know you plan to do that if you've made it this far. I hope that your corgi brings you many smiles.